The
Reflective Life

"When it comes to sensitized living, Ken is a master. I've watched him do life through its best and worst, and I can assure you that when it comes to the art of hearing God, he has it to give away. He is not only a master 'listener,' he is also a master communicator . . . an author with a potent arsenal of stories, images, and exquisitely crafted words to make it a joy to listen and learn."

Roc Bottomly, pastor,
Bridgeway Church,
Edmond, Oklahoma

REFLECTIVE LIVING SERIES

The
Reflective Life

*Becoming More Spiritually Sensitive
to the Everyday Moments of Life*

KEN GIRE

Chariot Victor Publishing
A Division of Cook Communications

Chariot Victor Publishing
A division of Cook Communications, Colorado Springs, Colorado 80918
Cook Communications, Paris, Ontario
Kingsway Communications, Eastbourne, England

An effort has been made to locate sources and obtain permission, where necessary for the quotations
used in this book. In the event of any unintentional omission, a modification will gladly be incorporated
in future printings.

Editor: Greg Clouse
Cover and Interior Design: D² DesignWorks
Cover Photo: Richard Hamilton Smith

1 2 3 4 5 6 7 8 9 10 Printing/Year 02 01 00 99 98

CIP applied for

CONTENTS

Introduction 9

I. THE REFLECTIVE LIFE 13

II. THE SEED OF THE REFLECTIVE LIFE 39

III. THE SOIL OF THE REFLECTIVE LIFE 51

IV. THE WATER OF THE REFLECTIVE LIFE 61

V. THE CULTIVATION OF THE REFLECTIVE LIFE 73

VI. THE GROWTH OF THE REFLECTIVE LIFE 105

VII. THE FRUIT OF THE REFLECTIVE LIFE 159

VIII. THE HARVEST OF THE REFLECTIVE LIFE 169

Endnotes 177

Appendix A 183
Reflections on the Word Devotional

Appendix B 197
Reflections on Your Life Journal

Appendix C 219
Recommended Books to Nurture the Reflective Life

WITH AN ETERNITY OF GRATITUDE

I DEDICATE THIS BOOK TO

SCOTT MANLEY.

WHEN YOU, THE READER, FINISH IT,

YOU'LL UNDERSTAND WHY.

INTRODUCTION

Ah done pass'a missa lye.

Ah know'n missa law.

Ma' lilten kine a'fu wi'enja.

Inna tye'a shie done come Tizrah.

Inna tye'a feliss, done come feliss.

The cryptic words come from the movie, *Nell,* whose central character is played by Jodie Foster. After her mother dies, Nell grows up alone in the forest, where she knows little of the world's influences and none of its conveniences.

She knows nothing of electricity or plumbing or refrigerators, nothing of television or radio or films, nothing of wars or politics, sports or fashions, nothing of the world beyond the forest.

But then the world beyond the forest discovers her. She is befriended and studied, and at last taken out of the forest by well-meaning authorities who feel she should catch up with the rest of the world so she can lead a fuller and richer life. Her fate finally falls into the hands of twelve jurors. After the lawyers on both sides finish their closing arguments, Nell gets up to speak for herself, addressing the jury in the primitive speech she learned as a young child.

"Yo' ha' erna lay—" she says.

"You have big things," another woman translates.

"Yo know'n erna lay—"

"You know big things—"

Nell leans toward the jury, gripping the rail that separates them. *"Ma' you' nay seen inna alo'sees—"*

"But you don't look into each other's eyes."

The intensity of her voice rises. *"An yo' aken of'a lilta-lilt."*

"And you're hungry for quietness."

The indictment registers on the faces of the jurors. Nell takes a breath as she searches for the right words. *"Ah done pass'a missa lye—"*

"I've lived a small life—"

"Ah know'n missa law."

"And I know small things."

Nell turns from the jury, looking into the eyes of the judge, then into the eyes of those in the courtroom, desperately trying to get them to understand. *"Ma' lilten kine a'fu wi'enja—"*

"But the quiet forest is full of angels—"

"Inna tye'a shie done come Tizrah—"

"In the daytime there comes beauty—"

"Inna tye'a feliss, done come feliss."

"In the nighttime, there comes happiness."

Every eye in the courtroom is riveted on her as she pauses, gathering her words like eggs from a nest. *"Nay tata fo' Nell."*

"Don't be afraid for Nell."

"Nay kee fo' Nell."

"Don't weep for Nell."

"Ah hai' nay erna keena'n you."

"I have no greater sorrows than yours."[1]

In the backwoods with her bare feet and broken speech, Nell lived a small life, knowing only small things. She knew nothing of stock prices or cellular phones, nothing of the state of the union or the scandals of its leaders, nothing of the mysteries of the universe or the miracles of modern science.

Yet her nights were filled with happiness, her days with beauty, and she sensed something of the divine in the world around her.

Nell was right.

We shouldn't weep for her. We should weep for ourselves. For we have big things, know big things, yet our nights are filled with anxiety, our days with drudgery, and in the forest around us we see only trees.

We have big things—megachurches, multimedia resources, ministries that reach around the world. We know big things—the doctrines of the Bible, the differences between the denominations, the dateline to Armageddon.

But we don't look into each other's eyes.

And we're hungry for quietness.

We're starved for a life that not only senses the sacred in the world around us but savors it. We're famished for experiences that are real, relationships that are deep, work that is meaningful.

I think what we're longing for is not "the good life" as it's been advertised to us in the American dream, but life in its fullness, its richness, its abundance. Living more reflectively helps us enter into that fullness.

The reflective life is a life that is attentive, receptive, and responsive to what God is doing in us and around us. It's a life that asks God to reach into our heart, allowing Him to touch us there, regardless of the pleasure it excites or the pain it inflicts. It's a life that reaches back, straining to touch the hem of Christ's garment, allowing Him to turn and call us out of the crowd, regardless of how humiliating it is to stand before Him or how uncertain we are as to what He will say. Uncertain whether He will say, "O you of little faith" or "Your faith has made you well." Uncertain whether He will say, "Follow me" or "Where I am going you cannot follow."

Regardless of the uncertainty, we can be certain of this. The words He speaks are words of life. That is why we *must* reach for them, receive them, and respond to them. Whatever they may say, however they may sound, whatever implications they may have for our lives, the words that proceed from His mouth offer life to our soul.

Those words are how our relationship with God grows.

Living reflectively is how we receive them.

PART I

The Reflective Life

Over the margins of life comes a whisper, a faint call, a premonition of richer living which we know we are passing by. Strained by the very mad pace of our daily outer burdens, we are further strained by an inward uneasiness, because we have hints that there is a way of life vastly richer and deeper than all this hurried existence, a life of unhurried serenity and peace and power.[1]

THOMAS KELLY
A Testament of Devotion

The Sacredness of Life

Our life is not our own property but a possession of God. And it is this divine ownership that makes life a sacred thing.[1]

ABRAHAM HESCHEL

Man Is Not Alone: A Philosophy of Religion

The phone call was from a stranger.

She had read a children's book I had written and was wondering if I would look at a project of hers. She told me a little about the story, which centered around a family of bears. She also told me about having had her pancreas removed because of cancer, and that she had several young children and thought that maybe God was prompting her to write the book for them. I agreed to look at it and offer any help I could.

After the manuscript arrived in the mail, I read it, then went about the work of making notes in the margins, crossing out some of the words, adding transitions, rearranging some of the paragraphs, basically the same type of thing I do with the rough drafts of my own work.

We met for breakfast. She brought her satchel with a sheaf of papers. I brought her manuscript with a scribble of suggestions. As we ordered, I asked about her health. She mentioned the cancer had spread to her liver, but that the doctors were watching it. The conversation small-talked around other things. She was in her mid-thirties, and she thought that since all her kids were now in school, it might be a good time to start writing. After the food arrived, I took out her manuscript, giving my initial reactions before doing a page-by-page analysis. She listened intently as I read my notes from the margin.

She listened so intently I hardly noticed her taking out a little kit with a shot and a vial of insulin. My father had been a diabetic and also insulin dependent, so I had seen this plenty of times. Still, it always made me a little queasy. She proceeded to inject herself, and out of politeness I ignored it, continuing my commentary.

Slowly, though, the blood drained from my words. The more I talked, the more pale and anemic those words sounded.

Then it dawned on me. The woman had her pancreas taken out because of cancer and now the cancer has spread to her liver. *She's dying.* She's dying, and she's wanting to write this book as a legacy for her children, something she can leave behind, maybe to help support them, or maybe simply to remind them . . . that once upon a time they had a mother.

I was doing this woman a disservice by critiquing the words she had written. A terrible disservice. But thank God, I realized it and stopped. I lowered the manuscript to the table. And this writer, this professional writer who makes his living with words, struggled to find ones that were even close to adequate.

"Please forgive me," I said. "I don't want to hurt your feelings. But . . . *this* is not what you should be writing," I said, touching the manuscript. "Not now. Not at this time in your life."

I drew a deep breath, hoping more words would come. "I'm not a doctor," I said, "but what you have is very, very serious. And there is a real possibility you won't be here to see your children grow up."

Her eyes pooled with tears. So did mine.

I took another breath. "No one will be able to take your place in their lives. Your husband may marry again, but no one will be able to fill the 'mother hole' in your kids' lives. There will be words they need to hear to help fill that hole. Words only you can say. Write *those* words. Write a letter to each of them for when they graduate from high school, telling them how proud you are of them and how sorry that you couldn't be there. When they go off to college, have a letter that can go with them. And when they get married."

It broke my heart to say those words.

It broke hers to hear them.

They were not the words I had prepared to say, nor the ones she had prepared to hear. But I believe they were the words God wanted said, however hard it was for me to say them, and the ones He wanted heard, however hard it was for her to hear them.

The Sacredness of Our Neighbor

It was a book that brought the two of us together so that those words could be shared.

Books in a way are sacraments that make the communion between an author and a reader possible. The white paper and black ink are the means through which one heart is revealed to another. But the paper and the words are merely the elements of the sacrament. What is sacred is the heart that writes the book and the heart that sits in silent communion to take and read what has been written.

The words that are read are small, wafer-like things. But sometimes, on some page, God humbles Himself to come through some of those words and touch the reader's heart. It is not the words that are sacred but God who is sacred . . . and the person to whom He comes.

In a sermon C.S. Lewis once said that next to the Blessed Sacrament our neighbor is the holiest thing presented to our senses. Most of us, though, are oblivious to that holiness except at rare moments, like that moment at breakfast.

"The awe that we sense or ought to sense when standing in the presence of a human being is a moment of intuition for the likeness of God which is concealed in his essence," wrote the Jewish scholar Abraham Heschel. "Not only man; even inanimate things stand in relation to the Creator. The secret of every being is the divine care and concern that are invested in it. Something sacred is at stake in every event."[2]

Something sacred.

At stake.

In every event.

A sobering thought, if it's true. And if it's true, it changes everything. Every moment of our day, every day of our life. Every dinner with the family, every breakfast with a stranger.

In a moment of reflection the Holy Spirit got my attention and alerted me to the fact that something sacred was at stake that morning at breakfast. And it wasn't a manuscript. It was a person's life and how God was wanting to use that life in the lives of those she loved.

The Sacredness of Our Life

Something of the sacredness of life was also brought to my attention through a reflective moment in a used bookstore. It was not too long after I had seen the movie, *Dances with Wolves*, which had stimulated my interest in the culture of the American Indian. Browsing through the shelves, I came across a slender volume titled, *The Gospel of the Redman*, by Ernest Thompson Seton.

Written by a whiteman who had lived among the Indians, the book had insightful perspectives on both cultures, as indicated in the opening paragraph of the first chapter. "The culture and civilization of the Whiteman are essentially material; his measure of success is 'How much property have I acquired for myself?' The culture of the Redman is fundamentally spiritual; his measure of success is, 'How much service have I rendered to my people?'"[3]

Pretty poignant analysis, I thought. And pretty convicting.

I leafed through the yellowed pages and stopped at a story that illustrated the difference between those two cultures. It was titled simply, "The Old Onion Seller."

In a shady corner of the great market at Mexico City was an old Indian named Pota-lamo. He had twenty strings of onions hanging in front of him.

An American from Chicago came up and said:

"How much for a string of onions?"

"Ten cents," said Pota-lamo.

"How much for two strings?"

"Twenty cents," was the reply.

"How much for three strings?"

"Thirty cents," was the answer.

"Not much reduction in that," said the American. "Would you take twenty-five cents?"

"No," said the Indian.

"How much for your whole twenty strings?" said the American.

"I would not sell you my twenty strings," replied the Indian.

"Why not?" said the American. "Aren't you here to sell your onions?"

"No," replied the Indian. "I am here to live my life. I love this market place. I love the crowds and the red serapes. I love the sunlight and the waving palmettos. I love to have Pedro and Luis come by and say: 'Buenas dias' . . . and talk about the babies and the crops. I love to see my friends. That is my life. For that I sit here all day and sell my twenty strings of onions. But if I sell all my onions to one customer, then is my day ended. I have lost my life that I love—and that I will not do."[4]

I thought a lot about that story, about living life in such a way that valued community over commerce, and it seemed a more Christian way of life than I was living mine.

I thumbed the pages till I came to a section titled, "The Daily Worship," and it got even more convicting.

"In the life of an Indian," says Ohiyesa, the Sioux, "there is only one inevitable duty—the duty of prayer, the daily recognition of the Unseen and Eternal. His daily devotions were more necessary to him than daily food. He wakes at daybreak, puts on his moccasins, and steps down to the water's edge. Here he throws handfuls of clear, cold water into his face, or plunges in bodily. After the bath, he stands erect before the advancing dawn, facing the sun as it dances upon the horizon, and offers his unspoken orison. His mate may precede or follow him in his devotions, but never accompanies him. Each soul must meet the morning sun, the new sweet earth, and the Great Silence alone."[5]

When I finished reading those words, I thought about my life, reflecting on how I met the morning sun each day, on what the one inevitable duty of my life was, on how necessary my daily devotions were to me. And it seemed to me that the Indian was the more civilized and I the more primitive one.

That book, which God brought to my attention in a few moments of reflection, made me think long and hard about life in general and my own life in particular.

The life we have been given can't be bought or bargained for. It is a gift. Every good and perfect gift comes from above, James tells us, coming down from the Father of lights in whom there is no variation or shifting shadow (1:17). If our day is indeed a gift from God, something of the Giver should be evident within that gift.

Abraham Heschel said, "There is a unique kind of transparence about things and events. The world is seen through, and no veil can conceal God completely. So the pious man is ever alert to see behind the appearance of things a trace of the divine, and thus his attitude toward life is one of expectant reverence."[6]

It is a great loss that we awake to so many gifts on a given day, not only without opening them, but without knowing they are even there for us to open. When each of us awakes, it should be with a splash-of-cold-water-in-the-face awareness that it has been given me another day to live. To *me*. To others that gift has been withheld. The sun rises, but their eyes will forever be closed to its light, its beauty, its blessings. But to me another day, for whatever reason, has been given. Another day to give gifts and to receive them. To love and to be loved. To embrace God through the moments of my day, and through those moments to be embraced by Him.

Each new morning that God's mercies dawn on us with the gift of another day, we should greet that day with an attitude of expectant reverence, as one kneeling to receive the sacrament of some holy communion, for truly it is.

The Sacredness of Our Communion with God

The sacraments of my childhood were peanut butter and jelly, cookies and milk, and sugarbread.

The giving and receiving of sugarbread was a midafternoon ritual. The screen doors of summer flying open, slapping shut. A barefoot boy bounding in from play, bent over with sudden hunger, begging for something to eat. An aproned mother pausing in the kitchen to fix something sweet for her out-of-breath son.

Sugarbread was a slice of white bread with a smear of margarine and a sprinkling of sugar. It was soft and sweet and somehow filled a greater hunger than bread alone ever could. Someone once said that if we bake bread without love, we nourish only half the person. The other half of the sugarbread was the love that went with it. It was given with a smile and a pat on the head and somehow that made it all the more filling.

As a playworn child, I depended on it to get me through the day. As a workworn adult, I depend on it still. Only now it's not the sugarbread. It's the memory of sugarbread. The memory that I was someone for whom a grown-up took time to take care of. The memory that I was looked after and loved.

Sacraments are ordinary things through which something extraordinary is offered. An ordinary bush ablaze with God's glory. Tablets of earthly stone engraved by a heavenly hand. The divine Word becoming flesh and dwelling among us.

As I page through those ancient stories from the sunken ease of my living room chair, it is not hard for me to hear in them the echo of God's voice. But can I hear Him now, speaking not to Moses or to David but to *me?*

Should we even expect Him to speak in the everyday moments of our lives? Or should we be content with echoes, however eloquent, from the past?

If God does still speak, perhaps some of those words are words for us. Perhaps He is offering us in the midafternoons of our lives small slices of heaven to stave off the hunger—or maybe to arouse it.

Something from heaven offered to us through earthly hands.

Coming to us like a sacrament.

Letting us know that we are looked after and that we are loved.

Slowing Down to See
What Is Sacred

Those who have abandoned themselves to God always lead mysterious lives and receive from him exceptional and miraculous gifts by means of the most ordinary, natural and chance experiences in which there appears to be nothing unusual. The simplest sermon, the most banal conversations, the least erudite books become a source of knowledge and wisdom to these souls by virtue of God's purpose. This is why they carefully pick up the crumbs which clever minds tread under foot, for to them everything is precious and a source of enrichment.[1]

JEAN-PIERRE DE CAUSSADE

The Sacrament of the Present Moment

M uch of what is sacred is hidden in the ordinary, everyday moments of our lives. To see something of the sacred in those moments takes slowing down so we can live our lives more reflectively.

The word *reflect* comes from two Latin words: *re*, meaning "back," and *flectere*, meaning "to bend." To reflect, then, is to bend back something, like the way a mirror bends back an image, providing an opportunity for a closer look. Living reflectively provides opportunities during our day for a closer look at things, at people, at ourselves, and at God. The faster the pace of our life, though, the more we will miss those opportunities.

The speed limit on I-25—the highway near where I live that runs parallel to the Front Range of the Rocky Mountains—is 75 miles per hour, and with all the traffic on the highway, slowing down is not easy. On most days when I'm driving the highway I'm staring blankly at the road ahead, but on some days the corner of my eye catches an angle of sun falling on the foothills that causes me to slow down. It may be familiar terrain, terrain I pass every day, but there is something about *this* day and the way the clouds part to pour light on a bare outcropping of rock or a stand of aspen or a common meadow that compels me to pull the car off the side of the road to take it all in.

Along that stretch of road I've seen slated hand-fans of the sun's rays spread across a Sistine Chapel ceiling of sky. On some nights, I've spotted meteors streaking the sky that are so spectacular I can actually see sparks spraying off of them. On some days, I've seen snow on the branches that has crystallized in such a magical way I feel as if I've fallen through the back of some wardrobe leading to Narnia. And I've seen double-rainbows, arching from one end of the landscape to another, that makes me think for a moment that maybe I've been swept away to the land of Oz.

It seems there should be moments like that in our spiritual lives, too. "In every man's life there are moments when there is a lifting of the veil at the horizon of the known, opening a sight of the eternal," noted Abraham Heschel. "To some people they are like shooting stars, passing and unremembered. In others they kindle a light that is never quenched."[2]

I wish for you such moments, as I wish them for me. I wish them the way a child wishes for Oz and Narnia, with the clandestine hope we all have inside us for heaven. To see them, though, we have to slow down. And to take them in, we have to stop.

The Sacredness of Human Life

There are many things that cause us to slow down and stop so we can reflect on our life. Sometimes a phone call does it. This particular phone call was from another stranger. I was at work at the time. The woman introduced herself with the fewest of words, saying she was calling on behalf of my publisher. "I'm afraid I have bad news for you," she said.

And in the split second between that sentence and the next, I thought, *Oh no, one of my books is going out of print.*

Her next sentence was: "Your editor, Nia Jones, has been killed in a car accident."

Stunned, I closed my eyes as she filled my silence with details of the crash. "She was driving through a construction site yesterday, and an earth-moving machine ran over the front half of the car, crushing her and killing her instantly. Her five-year-old son was buckled in the backseat, but he escaped unharmed."

Nia was my editor for *Intimate Moments with the Savior, Incredible Moments with the Savior,* and *The Gift of Remembrance.* We talked on the phone and corresponded, but I never met her, never knew what she looked like. I knew her only by the sound of her voice over the phone. Whenever she called, we talked mainly about editorial things, book things, work-related things. Occasionally, though, we talked about our lives.

She told me about her kids. I told her about mine. She told me how she wanted to go back to teaching so she could have the summers off to spend more time with them. Ten days before the accident she quit her job at the publishing company to do just that. She was on her way to pick up her last paycheck when the accident happened.

After the phone call ended, I cried for probably twenty minutes. I gave my work to my assistant editor, told her what happened and that I was leaving for the day. When I got home, my daughter Gretchen met me at the door. She asked why I was home early. I hugged her and clinged to her as I told her through my tears. I went to my bedroom where I rested on the bed, staring at the ceiling, tears spilling warmly across my face. I thought about a lot of things as I rested there. I thought about how congenial Nia was to work with. How good she was at her craft. How proud she had been of my books. She received no credit for them and only workman's wages for remuneration. But that didn't matter to her. All that mattered was that the work was good. And it struck me, for the first time, what a servant she was . . . what a true servant.

I flew to Michigan, where the funeral was held. Once there, I picked up a copy of the local newspaper, and on the front page was the story of the accident and a photograph of the massive earth-moving machine resting on Nia's crumpled car. At the funeral I met some of her coworkers, her husband, her young kids, and the sadness of it all was overwhelming.

She was so young. She had so much to live for. She was leaving her job for such a good reason, to spend more time with her kids. And suddenly, without warning, that time with her kids came to an untimely end.

It is better to go to the house of mourning than the house of feasting, said Solomon, because that is where we will all end up some day, and the wise take it to heart (Ecclesiastes 7:2-4). The pause that the funeral put in my schedule gave me plenty of time to reflect, not only on Nia's life but on my own.

I knew Nia only as my editor, but she was so much more than that. She was some man's wife, some children's mother, some brother's sister, some mother's and father's daughter. And though her vacancy at work could be filled by somebody else, what somebody could fill the vacancies in the hearts of those she left behind?

When a book goes out of print, it's not a big loss to the world, but when a mother dies, the world for some is never the same again. We stop to recognize such losses when we take time off to attend a funeral. And it's there, in the house of mourning, that we are reminded about what's really important in life. In those moments we realize that it is not the work we do that is so important. It's the people we work with. It's the work God does in our lives through them. And it's the work He does in their lives through us. That is what's sacred. Slowing down and stopping is our way of acknowledging it.

The Sacredness of All Life

A poignant illustration of this can be found in the opening scene of the movie, *The Last of the Mohicans*, starring Daniel Day-Lewis. Lewis and two Indians are running through a thickly wooded forest, muskets in hand, as the soundtrack quickens to keep pace with their bounding strides. We don't know what they're chasing, but we feel our own adrenaline pumping in the pursuit. Then we see it, a majestic elk running through the forest. Lewis stops, gets the elk in his sights, and fires.

The instant he does, the filmmaker uses a subtle, almost subliminal technique. For a second or two after the shot is fired, the film speed slows.

29

The breakneck pace of the hunt comes to an abrupt stop. So does the soundtrack. The three men stand still, then slowly make their way down the ravine where the elk has fallen. Within several feet of the animal, they stop. The older Indian offers a prayer. "We're sorry to kill you, Brother." He pauses a moment to catch his breath, then continues. "We do honor to your courage and speed, your strength." The other Indian bends down, the light from the forest catching the sadness in his face, and he brings a hand to his cheek as if to wipe away a tear.

The sense of life's sacredness permeates the scene. No one is laughing or joking or high-fiving each other. No one is bragging about the excitement of the chase or the precision of the shot or the size of the rack. A life has been sacrificed so that other lives could be sustained. And though the loss was necessary, a sense of the loss was felt by all, mourned by all, honored by all.

We didn't always live on animal life, according to the Bible. Only after the Flood were we given permission to eat meat.

And God blessed Noah and his sons and said to them, "Be fruitful and multiply, and fill the earth. And the fear of you and the terror of you shall be on every beast of the earth and on every bird of the sky; with everything that creeps on the ground, and all the fish of the sea, into your hands they are given. Every moving thing that is alive shall be food for you; I give all to you, as I gave the green plant" (Genesis 9:1-3).

When I reflect on when Noah and his sons first hunted animals, first skinned them, first cleaned them, first ate them, I wonder how they felt about it all. About taking an innocent animal's life to sustain their own. And I think about that first scene in *The Last of the Mohicans*, and it seems the

Indians are closer to that feeling than we.

The year their story took place was 1757. The place, North America. Since then, two hundred some odd years have passed. So have the last of the Mohicans. The Iroquois. The Sioux. And something else. The sense that there is something of eternal significance in everything around us, something that calls out not simply to be recognized but to be revered. That has passed, too.

Who of us even thinks about the sacrifice made to sustain us when we put a steak into our grocery cart, let alone feel anything close to the remorse those Indians felt?

The Indians, primitive as they were, seemed in touch with what was sacred. And we, civilized as we are, seem so out of touch. Maybe the reason for the difference is in the way we relate to the world. We can objectify the world or sanctify it. When we objectify the world, we view it and all that is in it as existing solely for our use, whether that use is for pleasure or profit or patriotism. When we sanctify the world, we view it and all that is in it with appreciation. In doing so, we recognize them not simply as objects, but as objects created by God that in some way reflect Him and all that is dear to Him, the way a work of art in some way reflects the artist and what is dear to the artist's heart.

Manipulation, whether it's of people or animals or things, originates from the arrogance of takers. Appreciation, on the other hand, stems from the humility of caretakers. Of the two ways of viewing the world, the one that most reflects the image of God is the caretaker. For God cares for the world He created, from the rising of a nation to the falling of the sparrow. Everything in the world lies under the watchful gaze of His providential eyes, from the numbering of the days of our life to the numbering of the hairs on our head. When we look at the world from that perspective, it produces within us a response of reverence. The loss of reverence has profound consequences. "Let your conceit diminish your ability to revere," wrote Abraham Heschel, "and the universe becomes a market place for you."[3]

For many who came to America, the new world became just that. A marketplace. Land for the taking. Buffalo for the skinning. Gold for the panning. It was all there. All you had to do was take it. Where they took it was from the Indians. The Indians, they thought, were little more than animals, and their scalps little more than trophies from the hunt. It should come as no surprise, then, when we happen upon this gravestone of a seventeenth-century Puritan:

> *Sacred to the Memory*
> *of*
> *Lynn S. Love*
> *who, during his life time, killed 98 Indians that had been*
> *delivered into his hands by the Lord. He had hoped to*
> *make it 100 before the year ended when he fell asleep in*
> *the arms of Jesus in his home,*
> *In N.Y. State* [4]

It is hard to imagine that those who call Jesus their Lord would take pride in such things, just as it is hard to imagine that some Christians proudly owned slaves, proudly discriminated against women, proudly persecuted Jews. But they did. They bought and sold them, used them and discarded them, as if they were commodities.

In pre-Nazi Germany it was a common saying that "the human body contains a sufficient amount of fat to make seven cakes of soap, enough iron to make a medium-sized nail, a sufficient amount of phosphorus to equip two thousand match-heads, enough sulphur to rid one's self of one's fleas."[5] By reducing the sacredness of a human being to its physical components, the Nazis justified themselves in making whatever use of them they could, whether for soap or for slaves. During the war, Himmler told his SS generals: "Whether the other nations live in prosperity or starve to death interests me only in so far as we need them as slaves for our culture. . . . Whether 10,000 Russian females fall down from exhaustion while digging an anti-tank ditch or not interests me only in so far as the anti-tank ditch for Germany is finished."[6]

There is more to you and me than the value of our physical components. There is more to us than the service we perform. More to us than what people see on the surface.

"I am not an animal," cried John Merrick in the movie, *The Elephant Man*. The mob that chased him through a London train station and cornered him in a restroom saw only the grotesqueness of his physical deformities. But something inside him protested. "I am not an animal. I . . . am . . . a . . . human . . . being."

That is the cry of the human soul. And every one of us at some time or another has cried it. I am *not* an employee. I am *not* a maid. I am *not* a meal ticket. I am *not* a sex object. I am *not* an athlete.

I am *not* an animal.

I . . . am . . . a . . . human . . . being.

I have a heart and a soul and a mind. I have hopes and dreams and feelings. I have been created in the image of God. He knows my name, hears my prayers, loves me. And He has hopes and dreams and feelings for me, too.

The Sacredness of a Child's Life

I heard a cry like that one evening from my daughter. She had returned from a party at a friend's home, where a bunch of kids from her school had come to watch the Super Bowl. The front door was locked, and she rang the doorbell. When I opened the door, it framed what looked to me a full-length portrait of sadness.

"How was the party?" I asked.

"Okay," she said, her eyes turned downward.

"Are you okay?" I asked. She nodded. "You sure?" She nodded again and went downstairs to her room.

I could see, even on the surface, that inside she was hurting. I could also see that she didn't want to talk, not then anyway. Later that evening she came to the kitchen, where my wife and I were, and fixed herself a bowl of ice cream. When I put my arm around her and asked how she was doing, she burst into tears. And through her tears, she said:

"Nobody at school likes me."

"That's not true," I said, trying to console her. "Lots of people like you."

"No they don't. No one talks to me. And whenever they do, I can tell they just feel sorry for me, feel they have to say something when they see me in the hall. But I know they don't really want to. I've been there two years, and nobody wants to get to know me. Nobody."

I held her as she cried. It broke our hearts to hear those words, to see this precious person we loved reduced to tears, feeling so worthless and so hopeless. After a few minutes, the tears ran their course and dried.

When they did, my wife and I talked with her about the rejection Christ went through when He came to earth. Even in His hometown. Even from His friends, His own family. He had so much inside He wanted to share. But so many people didn't want to hear, didn't have the time, didn't care about looking beneath the surface, had other places to go, other people in their lives who were more important, more interesting. Part of the Savior's suffering, we told her, involved rejection. It involved people ignoring Him, turning their backs on Him, walking away from Him. Through the rejection at school, she had entered in to what the Bible calls "the fellowship of His suffering." Although the rejection was mild in comparison to His, through it our daughter felt something of the Savior's pain when He walked this earth, something of His loneliness, something of His sadness. She was learning things about Christ that she could never learn in a school where she was the most popular kid. And what she learned would help her understand Him more, appreciate Him more, and love Him more.

The words seemed to help. We told her she could have the next day off from school, if she wanted to. And she did. By now, she was feeling better, and she asked if I wanted to sit in the hot tub with her out on the deck. "I'd like that," I said. As we warmed in the tub under the shivering stars, I told her about what my life as a writer was like. I told her what it was like to work hard at writing something, putting my heart into it, and then getting it back after several months with a form letter, saying things like "It's not a right fit for our publishing list, but best of luck placing it with some other publisher."

When you get a letter like that, I told her, you wonder if they read it, if they even took the time to skim it. There was so much you wanted to say in the manuscript, but people were too busy to read it, or didn't recognize the name on the manuscript and dismissed it, passing you by with a polite but impersonal wave: "Best of luck placing it with some other publisher."

I told her what it felt like to be rejected like that, how it still hurts, even after all these years as a professional writer. My entering in to something of her suffering opened a door that enabled her to enter in to something of mine. And there was fellowship there, in the sharing of our suffering. And there was a deeper sense of understanding that hadn't been there before. And a deeper sense of the sacredness, not only of the other person but of the other person's pain and the divine role that pain was playing in shaping that person into the image of Christ.

My daughter got out of the water and sat on the edge of the tub to cool off. Then she asked a question that forced my whole system of values to come out of hiding.

"What are you doing tomorrow?"

It wasn't a question really. It was an invitation. She was asking me to spend the day with her, but she didn't want me to feel the pressure to do it if I were too busy. Which I was. I was behind in my work and feverishly trying to catch up. But suddenly catching up didn't seem all that important. Not at the moment anyway. I knew something sacred was at stake in that moment. And though I didn't know exactly what it was, I knew what it wasn't. It wasn't my work.

"I don't think it's fair that you should be the only one to get a day off," I said. "Why don't we both take off, spend the whole day together. What do you say?"

"I'd like that," she said, and her face beamed.

"Me, too."

Then, as she stepped out of the hot tub and reached for a towel, she said, "Ya know, Dad, this is one of those memories I'll treasure the rest of my life."

The next day we didn't talk about anything in particular, certainly nothing life-changing. We just spent the day together and had fun. We went to the car wash, ran a few errands, ate lunch. We went to the mall, where she bought a pair of sunglasses. At the mall we saw a movie. *Sabrina*, with Harrison Ford. Then we went home.

All that day I thought about her words the night before. I think about them still.

"Ya know, Dad, this is one of those memories I'll treasure the rest of my life."

You would think those words made me feel like Father-of-the-Year. Just the opposite. As I reflected on what she said, I thought to myself, *I came so close to missing that time with her, missing making a memory that my daughter would treasure the rest of her life. And I realized how many times like that I* had *missed over the years. Not just with her but with the other kids, with my wife, my friends, other members of my family.* And the loss of those times, the loss of those moments in the lives of the people I loved and in my own life, made me sad.

It also made me determined. To slow down, so I can see when those moments present themselves. To stop, so I can honor them. To respond, so I would not pass by those moments without in some way touching them and without them in some way touching me.

Too many of those moments have passed me by.

I don't want to miss any more of them.

Life's too short.

And too sacred.

PART II

The Seed of the
Reflective Life

Every moment and every event of every man's life on
earth plants something in his soul. For just as the wind
carries thousands of invisible and visible winged seeds, so
the stream of time brings with it germs of spiritual vitality that come to rest imperceptibly in the minds and wills
of men. Most of these unnumbered seeds perish and are
lost, because men are not prepared to receive them.[1]

THOMAS MERTON

Seeds of Contemplation

The reflective life is a way of living that prepares the heart so that something of eternal significance can be planted there. Who knows what seeds may come to us, or what harvest will come of them. But if our heart is not prepared to receive them, as Thomas Merton warned, most of those seeds will perish and be lost.

I'm sure that over the years untold numbers of seeds have landed on my heart, just as I'm sure that untold numbers have perished there. They have perished not so much, I think, because of a hardness of heart as much as a selectivity of heart.

I knew, for example, that the Scriptures were seeds which should be received into the heart and nurtured. I knew my seminary professors had some seeds worth receiving. And there was always something of value planted from the hand of a Sunday morning sermon. And from some books.

From their hands some significant seeds were sown into my heart, some of which I believe were words from God. But I received those words selectively, not knowing others were even there to receive. It wasn't until I became a writer that I began stooping to examine some of those other seeds.

Having no formal training as a writer and knowing no writers, I had to learn my craft pretty much on my own. I stopped, looked, and listened to the world around me for whatever it had to teach. I listened to everything. To art. To music. To nature. To movies. To literature. To other people. These all became my mentors, guiding me into a deeper relationship with the world around me.

Which eventually led to the world inside me.

Space for the Seed

The world inside me looked like something of a rough draft that God was in the process of revising. I squinted at the scribbles and the scratch-outs, trying to understand the character He was developing, trying to follow its sometimes convoluted plot line and decipher its sometimes indecipherable themes.

It was hard work, but after years of working at it, I have come to realize that we all have to work at it if we are to have a more meaningful experience with God and with the world around us.

In the process of learning how to write, I learned how important it was to put pauses in my writing. Pauses create spaces in the reader's heart so the words the writer has written have room to live. The same principle applies to any of the texts we read.

A good example of this can be found in the following text of Scripture:

But Jesus went to the Mount of Olives. And early in the morning He came again into the temple, and all the people were coming to Him; and He sat down and began to teach them. And the scribes and Pharisees brought a woman caught in adultery, and having set her in the midst, they said to Him, "Teacher, this woman has been caught in adultery, in the very act. Now in the Law Moses commanded us to stone a woman; what then do You say?"

And they were saying this, testing Him, in order that they might have grounds for accusing Him. But Jesus stooped down, and with his finger wrote on the ground.

But when they persisted in asking Him, He straightened up, and said to them, "He who is without sin among you, let him be the first to throw a stone at her."

And again He stooped down, and wrote on the ground.

And when they heard it, they began to go out one by one, beginning with the older ones . . . (John 1:1-9).

When Jesus stooped down to write something on the ground, He created a pause with His silence. Into that pause flowed the crowd's attention, preparing them for the words that followed.

"He who is without sin among you, let him be the first to throw a stone at her."

When Jesus stooped down again, He created another pause. This time, though, what flowed into the silence was the crowd's guilt.

The space we give words—whether those words are the text of Scripture or the texts of our daily lives—allows them a place to live in our hearts. Without creating spaces of time in our lives, we stunt whatever growth the words were meant to produce.

Believers throughout the Bible were used to putting pauses into their lives. They structured pauses such as set times for daily prayers, strict observances for weekly Sabbaths, and holy days that punctuated the year, such as Passover and Yom Kippur. This habit of structuring pauses made it easier for them to take spontaneous pauses during the day, which is so essential for living a reflective life.

We have been taught to pause over the words we read in the Scriptures, and in some measure to reflect upon them. We are often illiterate, though, to the many other words that call to us.

The Seed

Frederick Buechner describes such words in his book, *A Room Called Remember*. "Every once in a while," he writes, "life can be very eloquent. You go along from day to day not noticing very much, not seeing or hearing very much, and then all of a sudden, when you least expect it very often, something speaks to you with such power that it catches you off guard, makes you listen whether you want to or not. Something speaks to you out of your own life with such directness that it is as if it calls you by name and forces you to look where you have not had the heart to look before, to hear something that maybe for years you have not had the wit or the courage to hear."[2]

All of us at some time or another have had experiences like that. Often, though, we're in such a hurry or the voice is so hard to hear that we miss what is being said. That voice we have heard or barely heard is not as mystical as it sounds. In fact, it's thoroughly biblical. Solomon describes it in the Book of Proverbs.

Wisdom shouts in the street,
She lifts her voice in the square;
At the head of the noisy streets she cries out;
At the entrance of the gates in the city, she utters her sayings. (1:20-21)

Does not wisdom call,
And understanding lift up her voice?
On top of the heights beside the way,

Where the paths meet, she takes her stand;
Beside the gates, at the opening to the city,
At the entrance of the doors, she cries out:
"To you, O men, I call,
And my voice is to the sons of men.
O naive ones, discern prudence;
And, O fools, discern wisdom." (8:1-5)

"Blessed is the man who listens to me,
Watching daily at my gates,
Waiting at my doorposts.
For he who finds me finds life,
And obtains favor from the Lord." (vv. 34-35)

This voice that calls to us out of the everyday moments of life is called the wisdom of God. This wisdom is infused into nature and the laws that govern her (Proverbs 8:22-23, 29b-30a, and Job 38–41), and into human nature and the laws that govern it (Proverbs 5:1-23). In the proverbs quoted above, this wisdom is personified as a woman searching through the streets for anyone who will listen to her. For those who do, she has wealth to share that is more precious than gold, silver, or jewels (Proverbs 8:6-17).

The voice of wisdom may call to us from anywhere, from a side street to the town square. It may call to us through the busy traffic of our day or at some crossroads in our lives. We may hear the voice in a church or a movie theater, in a quiet moment by ourselves or in a noisy moment with thousands of others. But it is our name she is calling. And she is calling us to a different way of living.

The Hebrew word for *wisdom* means "the skill of living life." That skill is learned by cultivating habits of the heart that heighten our sensitivity to hearing God's voice, whether His words come to us generally in the form of universal wisdom or specifically in the form of personal revelation.

The Sower

In the Book of Proverbs, a book of universal wisdom, Solomon states that God's revelation goes beyond the universal to the personal. God, he tells us, "is intimate with the upright" (Proverbs 3:32). The word *intimate* means "private counsel." The Hebrew root means "to be tight, firm, pressed together," and one of its derivatives is the word for pillows or cushions, which are pressed together on a bed or couch. The derivative in Proverbs 3:32 means being pressed closely together for the purpose of confidential communication. The word is used of lovers whose heads lie pressed next to each other on pillows, where they reveal softly spoken intimacies with each other. The word is also used of friends who share their thoughts while sitting close together on a couch. In other places it is used of generals who convene under a tent and put their heads together to discuss battle strategy.

Personal relationships like these are sustained by mutual revelation. The more intimate the relationship, the more intimate the revelation. Take Abraham's relationship with God, for example. Abraham is called *what* in the Bible? "The *friend* of God." Because of God's friendship with him, it was only natural for God to want to reveal His plans about the destruction of Sodom, since some of Abraham's relatives lived there. "Shall I hide from Abraham what I am about to do?" God mused to Himself, then went on to reveal it (Genesis 18:17-21). Because of Abraham's friendship with God, it was also only natural for him to want to discuss those plans, revealing how he felt about them (vv. 22-33).

Turning to the New Testament, we see that the disciples had a similar relationship with Christ. "No longer do I call you slaves," Jesus told them in the upper room, "for the slave does not know what his master is doing; but I have called you friends . . ." (John 15:15). Jesus told them that if they were faithful in their friendship by loving Him and keeping His commandments, He would disclose Himself to them (John 14:21).

Most of us turned to Christ when we realized there was a difference between Christianity as a religion and Christianity as a relationship. Sometime after entering into that relationship with Christ, we realize something else. That there is a difference between a personal relationship with Christ and an intimate one. In any relationship, it is the depth of the relationship that determines the depth of our conversations within the relationship. Our conversation, for example, with a stranger we're standing next to in the grocery store line is different from our conversations with someone we've met before, which is different from our conversations with a friend, which is different from our conversations with a close friend, which is different from our conversations with our best friend or with our mate.

The same is true of our friendship with Jesus. Our level of intimacy within that relationship determines the depth of our conversations, both from us to Him and from Him to us.

Jesus discloses Himself to us in a variety of ways. Sometimes in gradual and unrecognizable ways that become increasingly clear, the way He did with the two disciples on the road to Emmaus (Luke 24:13-32). Sometimes in sudden and spectacular ways that are instantly clear, the way He did with Saul on the road to Damascus (Acts 9:1-9). And sometimes in obscure ways that won't be clear until the end of time, the way He does when He comes to us in the form of someone who in some way needs us (Matthew 25:31-46).

Jesus comes to us in a thousand ways and for a thousand reasons, all of them for our good. "Behold," He says, "I stand at the door and knock; if anyone hears My voice and opens the door, I will come in to him, and will dine with him, and he with Me" (Revelation 3:20). He comes knocking on the door of our heart, any time of the night or day, and to any of us who can recognize His voice through the thickness of the wood, He makes an amazing promise.

He promises us a meal.

Not a lecture on nutrition.

Not a reprimand about our eating habits.

A meal.

It is a meal of mutual fellowship. I will dine *with him,* and he *with Me.* It is also a meal of mutual nourishment. *He* will dine as well as we. The meal is not simply for us. It is for Him, too. When He comes to the door, however late He knocks, however lowly He appears in the doorway, it will be His presence that refreshes us and His words that nourish us.

People of faith wait up for that knock, anticipating His presence at their table and the words He has prepared for them to receive there. We have been taught to wait for Christ when He comes again in that one spectacular moment when everyone everywhere will at last recognize Him for who He is. And so we *should* look for him. But sometimes in looking ahead, we don't look anywhere else, and we miss all the other times He comes. For He is always coming. Coming to serve us, when we need it, the way He did with the disciples when He washed their feet (John 13:1-20), or with the watchful servants who waited up for Him (Luke 12:35-40). And coming to save us, when we need that, the way He saved Peter from drowning (Matthew 14:22-33), or the woman caught in adultery, who in another way was also drowning (John 8:1-11). He comes to save us from ourselves mostly, but from the world, the flesh, and the Devil, too. And since we're always in some way in need of saving, He is always in some way coming.

C.S. Lewis once said that our greatest dignity as creatures is not in initiative but in response. God speaks, we hear. He knocks, we open. He sows the seed, we receive it.

Sowing those seeds is God's attempt to restore Eden to the wilderness of the human heart.

Receiving them is how we work with Him to do it.

PART III

The Soil of the Reflective Life

This, my friend, is a secret of secrets. It will help you to reap where you have not sown, and it will be a continual source of grace in your soul. For everything that inwardly stirs in you, or outwardly happens to you, becomes a real good to you if it finds or excites in you *this humble state of mind.* For nothing is in vain, or without profit to the *humble soul.* It stands always in a state of divine growth; everything that falls upon it is like a dew of heaven to it.[1]

ANDREW MURRAY

Humility

If the Parable of the Sower teaches us anything, it teaches us this—that no matter how worthy the sower or how wonderful the seed, it is the condition of the soil that determines the crop (Matthew 13:1-23).

As the parable illustrates, the seed may fall on a heart that is packed hard from feet too hurried to stop and reflect on all that the seed has to offer. The seed may fall into a heart that is shallow in its understanding, and so the roots can't penetrate deeply enough for the plant to survive the inevitable scorch of difficult days ahead. The seed may fall into a heart that is overgrown with distractions, which seem harmless enough in the beginning but in the end choke out the growth. But if the seed falls into a heart that has been prepared, it will yield a harvest. Thirty. Sixty. In some cases, a harvest of a hundredfold.

Wouldn't it be wonderful to have a life like that, its barns full, its bushels running over, its bounty able to feed not only *our* family but to have enough left over to share with others? A life like that *would* be wonderful. But the soil from which it came wouldn't be.

To produce crops like that, the soil would have to be plowed, its clods broken up, its embedded resistance removed a rock at a time, the competing tendrils rooted out weed by weed. And to nourish the crops with the minerals they need, certain things in and around the soil would have to surrender their lives. Leaves. Twigs. Bark. Each in its own time and its own way would have to be broken off and fall to the ground. All of it would have to die and crumble into compost. Mixed with the manure left behind from passing animals. Rotted by the moisture and the mold and the mildew.

Mulched by insects. Eaten by bacteria. Stirred by the slow tunneling of earthworms.

Each of us wants a fruitful life, but who of us wants to go through *that* to get it?

The organic material that has been broken down to give the soil its richness is called "humus." Our word *humble* is related to it, meaning "to be brought low." That is the process God uses to makes us receptive to His word. He allows us to be brought low. Sometimes He Himself is the one who brings us there.

Humility, said Confucius, is the foundation of all virtues. Jesus said essentially the same thing when He placed the "poor in spirit" first in His list of beatitudes. The phrase would have brought to the mind of a Jewish audience the picture of someone who was down-and-out and desperate.

What is it like to be like that? It's like being on the street. Not knowing where your next meal's coming from. Not knowing where you're going to sleep tonight, or what dangers lie waiting when you do. It's not knowing what tomorrow holds, except more rejection, more sorrow, more hunger, more pain.

And *who* wants to live like that?

I, for one, do not. I want a roof over my head with a thirty-year guarantee on the shingles and a home-owner's policy to back it up. I want a door that closes out the world. A door with a lock. A lock with a deadbolt. And a deadbolt with a security system. I want a relationship with God, but without the risk. I want a religious fling, not a marriage I have to work at. I want the *Cliff Notes* to the faith, not the novel.

Who doesn't?

Who doesn't want to lick the filling from the Oreo? Who doesn't want the crust cut off the sandwich? Who doesn't want all that is sweet and soft about Christianity? Love. Joy. Peace.

Who of us wants to be men and women of sorrow, acquainted with grief?

Do any of us even know what that is like? To live with some pain that won't go away. To carry some heartache with us everywhere we go. To be hemmed in by sorrow. To be without a job, without the skills to get a job, without someone to help us get those skills. Do we know what it's like to be without money in the bank or under the mattress or anywhere else? With no assets. No collateral. Do we know what it's like to beg? Not to ask. Not to borrow. To beg.

The Weak and the Lowly

The beggars in Jesus' day were the loose ends of humanity that fringed the streets. The lame. The blind. The mentally ill. They were the Lazaruses set out on the curb like so much garbage. They were the Marys, limp dishrags of remorse, wringing tears from their twisted pasts, tears they used to wash the Savior's feet.

They were also the ones to whom Jesus preached His most famous sermon—the Sermon on the Mount.

Matthew says that when Jesus "saw the crowds, He went up on a mountainside and sat down," and then began to teach (5:1-2). Where did the crowds come from? Scroll-up to the preceding verse at the end of chapter four. "Large crowds from Galilee, the Decapolis, Jerusalem, Judea and the region across the Jordan followed Him" (4:25). And who made up these crowds? Scroll-up a couple of verses more. "And Jesus was going about in all Galilee, teaching in their synagogues, and proclaiming the gospel of the kingdom, and healing every kind of disease and every kind of sickness among the people. And the news about Him went out into all Syria; and they brought to Him all who were ill with various diseases and pains, demoniacs, epileptics, paralytics, and He healed them" (4:23-24).

The people crowding the front rows to hear that sermon were the ones Jesus had healed and delivered. Lepers. The demon-possessed. Epileptics. They were His audience. People who couldn't come to the temple. People who didn't dare darken the door of a synagogue. People who were outcasts, the unclean, the untouchables. People who had fallen among thieves. Robbed of their health. Stripped of their self-worth. Beaten down by life and left by the roadside.

They were the poor in spirit. Impoverished to the point of realizing that if they were to get their daily bread, they would have to beg. And with their tin cup extended toward heaven, that's just what they did.

"Son of David, have mercy on me."

"Give me this living water."

"God, be merciful to me, a sinner."

These people had been brought so low to the ground they didn't have anywhere to look but up. When our hands are that empty and extended toward heaven, begging for any crumbs that fall from the Master's table, then heaven will extend the grace for us to dine with Christ and Him with us.

We are told in the Scriptures that God gives grace to just such people, to people who have been brought low and humbled (James 4:6). If that is true, then whatever happens in our lives to humble us is, in the long run, a good thing, because it paves the road over which the grace of God comes to us.

The High and the Mighty

We are told in that same verse in James that God is opposed to the proud. The proud are not simply overlooked in the distribution of grace. They are opposed. And opposed not by just anybody. Opposed by God. Think of the utter futility of a life that has the mightiest power in the universe pitted against it.

Now think of this.

There is no pride God opposes as much as religious pride.

Think a moment about the scribes, the Pharisees, the teachers of the law. Think of their pride as guardians of the truth. Their pride as possessors of the promises of God. Their pride as pillars of the community, standing tall and straight in holding up the standards. Their pride in their obedience, their faithfulness, their good works. Remember the Pharisee praying in the temple? "God, I thank Thee that I am not like other people: swindlers, unjust, adulterers, or even like this tax-gatherer. I fast twice a week; I pay tithes of all I get" (Luke 18:11-12).

Now hear another prayer uttered in that same place. "But the tax-gatherer, standing some distance away, was even unwilling to lift up his eyes to heaven, but was beating his breast, saying, 'God, be merciful to me, the sinner!'" (v. 13)

Who knows what circumstances in the tax-gatherer's life came crashing down to bring him so low that he couldn't even look up. But whatever they were, the humility that resulted from them received Christ's approval. "I tell you," Christ commented, "this man went down to his house justified rather than the other; for everyone who exalts himself shall be humbled, but he who humbles himself shall be exalted" (v. 14).

"In humility," James says, "receive the word implanted, which is able to save your souls" (1:21). Trace the verse backwards.

The salvation of our souls.

The word implanted.

Our reception of that word.

Humility.

What is at the bottom of the list? Humility. Humility is what prepares the soil to be receptive so that it desperately clings to the word that has been planted in our heart. When the soil embraces the seed, it sets in motion a process of germination. When the soul allows the word to root deeply into its dark recesses, the word can take what is there and transform it not only into something vital but fruitful. Stop a moment and reflect on that. The welfare of our soul, not just its daily welfare but its eternal welfare, depends on the humility of our heart.

It's a staggering thought, even a terrifying thought. That the soil has such power. That heavenly words have been placed at the mercy of human hearts. To receive them or not to receive them. To feed their roots or to starve them. To nurture their growth or to choke it out. That the harvest of heaven depends on such earthly receptions is itself a picture of humility.

The proud are oblivious to such pictures. Their pride has placed them in a position where they can't even see that anything from heaven is being offered. Take Simon the Pharisee, for example (Luke 7:36-50). His hands were folded smugly against his chest as he looked down his nose at the prostitute weeping at Christ's feet. "If this man were a prophet," Simon reasoned to himself, "He would know what sort of person this woman is who is touching Him, that she is a sinner."

Jesus interrupted his thoughts. "Simon, I have something to say to you. A certain moneylender had two debtors: one owed five hundred denarii, and the other fifty. When they were unable to repay, he graciously forgave them both. Which of them therefore will love him more?"

Simon answered, "I suppose the one whom he forgave more."

"You have judged correctly," Jesus said. He then turned Simon's attention to the woman he had judged incorrectly. "Do you see this woman? I entered your house; you gave Me no water for My feet, but she has wet My feet with her tears, and wiped them with her hair. You gave Me no kiss; but she, since the time I came in, has not ceased to kiss My feet. You did not anoint My head with oil, but she anointed My feet with perfume. For this reason I say to you, her sins, which are many, have been forgiven, for she loved much; but he who is forgiven little, loves little."

Most of us, I think, genuinely want humility. But who of us is willing to be humiliated in order to get it? Yet it was the humiliation of this woman's moral failures that put her in a place to receive grace.

"Your sins have been forgiven," Jesus said to her. "Your faith has saved you; go in peace."

It is at the feet of Christ where we hear such words.

Humility is what brings us there.

And humility is what enables us to receive those words, giving them a fertile place in our heart to take root and to grow and to produce a harvest that only heaven knows how bountiful or how many harvests over the years it will seed in other people's lives.

PART IV

The Water of the Reflective Life

Germination is a strange process. It contains both death and life; like a new year, the old is cast aside, the new begins. The static perfection of the seed is thrown out of balance, undermined. Water seeps through husk and miracles occur. In arid Arizona after long wet winters the earth comes suddenly to life, and the desert blossoms. Seeds lying there dormant for many years waken to life laying purple blankets over vast slopes and painting hills with red and orange. Grain unearthed in dry Egyptian tombs planted in moist soil begin to swell and sprout. . . . From the seeds' constricted point of view, germinating is not a pleasant process. Penetrating through the shell, the water stirs activity. The germ of life is quickened, swells, begins to *live*.[1]

MORTON KELSEY

Prayer and the Redwood Seed

In the Parable of the Sower, Jesus compared the Word of God to seed, and the hearts upon which it falls, to soil. Without one key ingredient, though, the seed cannot germinate.

That ingredient is water.

What water is to the seed, the Spirit of God is to the Word of God. When the two come together in the human heart, a miracle happens. The seed springs to life.

The two forces worked in tandem at creation, the Spirit moving over the surface of the deep as a bird hovering over the eggs in its nest, working with the Word to bring form and fullness to the new earth (Genesis 1:2, Psalm 33:6). In the same way the Spirit works with the Word to germinate life in the new creation (John 3:5-8, James 1:18). The seeds of that new life are genetically coded to produce Christlikeness, again a cooperative work of God's Word and His Spirit (Romans 8:29, 1 Peter 1:22-23, Galatians 5:22-23).

That same cooperation is necessary for any word from God to take root in our lives. Take the inscripturated word, for example.

Anybody can read the Scriptures and understand at least something of what they have to say. With enough reference books, commentaries, and teaching, you can know *a lot* about what they have to say. You can know about the authors of the individual books and the specific issues they were addressing. You can know the historical context from which they wrote. You can know about the meanings of their words and the subtleties of their styles. You can even know theology.

What you can't know, apart from the Holy Spirit, is what those words mean to you personally at this particular juncture of your spiritual life. What can't happen apart from Him is that seed germinating and growing within you into the fullness of Christ.

In his book, *The Pursuit of God*, A.W. Tozer describes how the Holy Spirit germinates the Word of God in our hearts, then grows it, first the blade, then the ear, then the full ear. "It is important that we get still to wait on God. And it is best that we get alone, preferably with our Bible outspread before us. Then if we will we may draw near to God and begin to hear Him speak to us in our hearts. I think for the average person the progression will be something like this: First a sound as of a Presence walking in the garden. Then a voice, more intelligible, but still far from clear. Then the happy moment when the Spirit begins to illuminate the Scriptures, and that which had been only a sound, or at best a voice, now becomes an intelligible word, warm and intimate and clear as the word of a dear friend."[2]

Warm and intimate.

When Jesus said, "You shall know the truth, and the truth shall make you free" (John 8:32), He was not referring to an intellectual knowledge of the truth but an *intimate* knowledge. It's a knowledge that exists between lovers, the way Adam knew Eve (Genesis 4:1), and the way God knows each of us (Psalm 139:1-3).

The Spirit of Life

The difference between an intellectual approach to the Scriptures and an intimate approach is dramatized in a scene from *The Dead Poets Society*, starring Robin Williams as Professor Keating. One of my favorite scenes in the movie is a classroom scene where Keating calls on one of his students.

"Mr. Perry, will you read the opening paragraph of the preface: 'Understanding Poetry by Dr. J. Evans Pritchart, Ph.D.'?"

The young Mr. Perry opens his book and dutifully reads. "'To fully understand a poem we must be fluent in its meter, rhyme, and figures of speech. Then ask two questions: One. How artfully has the objective of the poem been rendered? Two. How important is that objective? Question one rates its perfection. Question two, its importance. Once these questions have been answered, seeing the poem's greatness is relatively easy. If the poem's score is plotted on a graph, with the vertical line representing its importance and the horizontal its perfection, its greatness can easily be ascertained.'"

As the boy continues to read, Keating chalks a graph on the blackboard. The other students carefully copy it in their notebooks. After Mr. Perry finishes, Keating turns to the class, smiles, then says one word.

"Excrement."

Which takes every student off guard.

"We're not laying pipe," says Keating with mounting passion. "We're talking about poetry. Now I want you to *rip out* that page. The entire page. Rip it out."

The students' eyes widen.

"In fact," Keating says, "rip out the *entire* introduction. I want it gone. History. Be gone, J. Evans Pritchart."

The students hesitate as they cut glances toward each other, wondering if this guy is for real.

"It's not the Bible," Keating assures them. "You're not going to hell."

One by one they start ripping, as Keating continues his impassioned plea.

"This is a battle, a war, and the casualties are our hearts and souls. Armies of academics going forward, measuring poetry. *No!* I'll not have that here. You're going to learn to think for yourselves, to savor words. No matter what anybody says, words and ideas can change the world."

Keating moves to the middle of the room and tells them all to huddle up. They're still not sure what's going on, but they move in around him because his passion is so real and so infectious.

"We don't read and write poetry because it's cute. We read and write poetry because we're members of the human race, and the human race is filled with passion. Medicine. Law. Business. Engineering. All noble pursuits and necessary to sustain life. But poetry, beauty, romance, love—these are what we stay alive for."

The story dramatizes the conflict between the ideals of the Classical Age and those of the Romantic Age. The educational institution embodies one set of ideals. The instructor, the other. The ideals of the school are etched in stone above its pillars: *Tradition. Honor. Discipline. Excellence.* Keating's ideas are enfleshed in his life: *Poetry. Beauty. Romance. Love.*

The conflict between Jesus and the religious establishment was over similar ideals. Chiseled into the thinking of the scribes and Pharisees were the ideals: *Law. Tradition. Ritual. Morality.* Into that establishment came a teacher with no formal education and a loyal following of disciples. He espoused things that sounded very much like: *Poetry. Beauty. Romance. Love.*

He told them, essentially, to rip out whatever human teachings or traditions were smothering their passion for God and for other people. They were not words He mouthed. They were words He lived. His passion was embodied in every prayer, every conversation, every healing, every pilgrimage to the temple.

There is a battle, a war, and the casualties could be our hearts and souls. The Christian life is about passion. Passion for God and passion for people in need. These are the words and ideas that when enfleshed can change the world. These are the things we live for.

But those things can easily get lost. One such way is by detaching them from the object of our love. When we do that, all we're left with are actions that only resemble love. Empty, impersonal acts. Like sex without love. And when sex is detached from love, it is reduced to technique. People may write handbooks on it, but not poetry.

All of us at some time or another have been guilty of approaching the Scriptures that way. Detaching it from the source of its life. Dissecting it in order to study it.

We study it as a handbook of principles, when we should see it as poetry.

We study it as a treatise on theology, when we should see it as beauty.

We study it as a record of biblical history, when we should see it as romance.

We study it as a code of conduct, when we should see it as love.

The Spirit of Love

Several years ago Ken Burns produced a series on the Civil War for PBS. He sifted through mounds of old photographs, letters, maps, diaries, historical records, and memoirs, editing them and adding sound effects and narration to put together a compelling documentary of that defining moment in

America's history. As Burns was doing his research, he came across a letter that captured the essence of what he wanted the series to show—the personal side of war. Here is that letter, written by Union Major Sullivan Ballou to his wife back home.

July 14, 1861
Camp Clark, Washington

My very dear Sarah:

The indications are very strong that we shall move in a few days—perhaps tomorrow. Lest I should not be able to write again, I feel impelled to write a few lines that may fall under your eye when I shall be no more. . . .

I have no misgivings about, or lack of confidence in the strong cause in which I am engaged, and my courage does not halt or falter. I know how strongly American Civilization now leans on the triumph of the Government, and how great a debt we owe to those who went before us through the blood and sufferings of the Revolution. And I am willing—perfectly willing—to lay down all my joys in this life, to help maintain this Government, and to pay that debt. . . .

Sarah my love for you is deathless, it seems to bind me with mighty cables that nothing but Omnipotence could break; and yet my love of Country comes over me like a strong wind and bears me unresistibly on with all these chains to the battle field.

The memories of the blissful moments I have spent with you come creeping over me, and I feel most gratified to God and to you that I have enjoyed them so long. And hard it is for me to give them up and burn to ashes the hopes of future years, when, God willing, we might have lived and loved together, and seen our sons grown up to honorable manhood around us. I have, I know, but few and small claims upon Divine Providence, but something whispers to me—perhaps it is the wafted prayer of my little Edgar, that I shall return to my loved ones unharmed. If I do not my dear Sarah, never forget how much I love you, and when my last breath escapes me on the battle field, it will whisper your name. Forgive my many faults, and the many pains I have caused you. How thoughtless and foolish I have often times been! How gladly I would wash out with my tears every little spot upon your happiness. . . .

But, O Sarah! if the dead can come back to this earth and flit unseen around those they loved, I shall always be near you; in the gladdest days and in the darkest nights . . . *always, always,* and if there be a soft breeze upon your cheek, it shall be my breath, as the cool air fans your throbbing temple, it shall be my spirit passing by. Sarah do not mourn me dead; think I am gone and wait for thee, for we shall meet again. . . . [3]

Sullivan Ballou died at the first battle of Bull Run.

This is what the war meant to so many people on both sides. Fathers who would not be coming home. Or sons. Families that would never be the same again. Wives who would be left to raise a family alone, plant crops alone, face an uncertain future alone. So he would never forget the reason why he was making the documentary, Burns folded the letter and kept it in his shirt pocket during the entire time he was working on the film.

We can use Sullivan Ballou's letter to study history, as a springboard to talk about the Civil War and the issues over which it was fought. We can use it to study geography, mapping out places like "Camp Clark, Washington," where the letter originated. We can focus on military references such as "the Revolution," and discuss the comparisons and contrasts between the two wars. We can do word studies, tracing the etymologies of such words as *wafted.* We can even use the letter to pursue theological studies, starting with American views on "Omnipotence" and "Providence," launching into discussions about which side of the war God was on.

In short, we can study the letter the way J. Evans Pritchart, Ph.D. studied poetry.

We can study the letter in its grammatical, historical context, but if we fail to understand it in the context of two people who have committed themselves in an intimate relationship with each other, we miss the point of the correspondence.

The whole point.

The same is true with the Bible. It is a factual, historical document, but if it's merely wars and dates we're concerned with, issues and lines of theological demarcation over which swords are drawn and battles are fought, we will miss the Person, who, from a faraway battlefield, has disclosed His heart to us. That last letter from Sullivan Ballou to his beloved wife Sarah sounds so much like some of the last words from Jesus to His disciples. In the intimate setting of the upper room, He told them in essence:

"I am going into battle soon. I don't want your heart to be troubled. It's love for my Father's country that sends me. I'm leaving, but I won't leave you alone. I'm going to send my Spirit to breeze across your brow when you need comfort . . . to whisper of my love. I shall always be near you . . . in the gladdest days and the darkest nights. And I go to prepare a place for you, to receive you to myself, that where I am you may be also . . . always . . . always" (see John 14–17).

Sullivan Ballou's letter has certain meaning for an historian, a slightly different meaning for a linguist, and an entirely different meaning for a film-maker. Each of those meanings is a valid perspective for study. But the ultimate meaning of the letter can only be found in the relationship of the lover to his beloved. That is the primary context by which all the words should be evaluated. It is the spirit of love existing between Sullivan and Sarah that gives the words life. Apart from that spirit, the words may educate me or enlighten me, even move me. But they will never pierce my heart the way they pierced Sarah's. They will never be treasured the way she treasured them. Or remembered the way she remembered them. And they won't be passed on the way she passed them on to her children.

The Bible is, first and foremost, a *love letter*. The words in that letter are like seeds that fall into the soil of our heart. With enough skill, we can precisely measure the seeds, weigh them, and study them. No amount of skill, though, can bring the seeds to life. Only the Holy Spirit can do that.

This is true of any word from God that lands in our heart—whether it's a word voiced through the Scriptures or through nature or through the circumstances of our lives. Each and every word that comes to us will lie dormant in the soil unless the Spirit gives it life.

And there it will wait . . . quiet and still . . . for the rain.

PART V

The Cultivation of the Reflective Life

Gardening forces you to be in the moment, to deal with what is happening in the here and now. Plants can't fake it like human beings can. They don't tell you everything is fine if it isn't. That's why observation is the single most useful talent to cultivate.[1]

JUDITH HANDELSMAN

Growing Myself: A Spiritual Journey Through Gardening

God's Mission Statement
for Our Life

The Constitution has endured and serves its vital function today because it is
based on correct principles, on the self-evident truths contained in the Declaration
of Independence. These principles empower the Constitution with a timeless
strength, even in the midst of social ambiguity and change. "Our peculiar securi-
ty," said Thomas Jefferson, "is in the possession of a written Constitution."

A personal mission statement based on correct principles becomes the same
kind of standard for an individual. It becomes a personal constitution, the basis
for making major, life-directing decisions, the basis for making daily decisions
in the midst of circumstances and emotions that affect our lives.[1]

STEPHEN R. COVEY

The 7 Habits of Highly Effective People

The reflective life is a way of living that heightens our spiritual senses to all that is sacred. The Scriptures are one of those sacred things. For the Jew, the most sacred passage in all the Scriptures is the *Shema* (pronounced *Shemmah,* with the accent on the last syllable). It is a transliteration of the Hebrew word meaning "hear," the first word in that most sacred passage.

"Hear, O Israel! The Lord is our God, the Lord is one! And you shall love the Lord your God with all your heart and with all your soul and with all your might" (Deuteronomy 6:4-5).

The *Shema* was the mission statement for believing Jews. It regulated every area of their lives, from work to worship. It was placed in the phylacteries they wore on their foreheads and within the Mezuzah they fastened to their doorposts. It was recited every morning and evening, and at the close of the most holy day, which is the Day of Atonement. It was also the last word breathed from the lips of the dying.

The command is the heart of the Old Testament. Somehow, though, the beat of that heart got drowned out by the incessant strum of lesser commands. Something like the simplicity of the Constitution getting lost in the library of legal cases that were meant to clarify it.

A lawyer looking for clarification asked Jesus, "Teacher, which is the great commandment in the Law?" Jesus answered by quoting the *Shema*. "'You shall love the Lord your God with all your heart, and with all your soul, and with all your mind.' This is the great and foremost commandment," Jesus explained. "And the second is like it, 'You shall love your neighbor as yourself.' On these two commandments depend the whole Law and the Prophets" (Matthew 22:34-40, see also Romans 13:8-10).

This vertical as well as horizontal orientation of our faith can be seen as far back as the giving of the Ten Commandments. The first four commandments, which were probably inscribed on the first tablet, deal exclusively with our relationship to God. The last six, which were probably inscribed on the second tablet, deal exclusively with our relationship to our neighbor. The two tablets stand in a cause-and-effect relationship to each other. If we love God, that love will naturally spill over into our relationships with people.

This same cause-and-effect relationship is the basis of John's argument in 1 John 4:20. "If someone says, 'I love God,' and hates his brother, he is a liar; for the one who does not love his brother whom he has seen, cannot love God whom he has not seen."

Before we can love our neighbor, we must *see* our neighbor and *hear* our neighbor. Observing the way a gardener observes plants. Watching their buds when they're blooming. Watering their roots when they're wilting. But we cannot weep with those who weep or rejoice with those who rejoice unless we first see something of their tears or hear something of their laughter. If we can learn to see and hear our neighbor, maybe, just maybe, we can learn to see and hear God. And seeing Him and hearing Him, to love Him.

To passionately love God and other people.

This is what matters.

This is *all* that matters.

And all that God requires.

But it requires our all to fulfill.

That is the mission statement, so to speak, of the reflective life. *Not to see better or to hear better but to love better.* To better love all that is sacred. And of all that is sacred, nothing is more sacred than God and the people He created as the object of His affection.

A Simple Mission Statement for Church

Sometimes something sacred happens in church that doesn't happen, perhaps *can't* happen, anywhere else. When it does, it's like a sudden angle of morning sun bringing the Bible story that is frozen in the stained-glass window to life.

I saw the stained-glass of Christ's words to the lawyer come to life one Sunday when my wife and I stumbled into a church that was different from what either of us before had attended. During worship I observed tears of love streaming down people's faces as they sang praises to Christ. Some people were sitting, others standing, still others kneeling. Some raised their arms in the air. Others lowered their faces to the floor.

After worship, the pastor got up to speak. He spoke to us like a father. His gestures weren't rehearsed. His sermon wasn't polished. But it was heartfelt and honest. After the service, the pastor and people from the staff prayed for anyone who wanted to be prayed for, and they stayed until every last person had been.

My wife and I found ourselves drawn back the next Sunday, where we continued to quietly observe what went on there. We learned that each day of the week one of the pastoral staff was on call at the church solely to meet the needs of those who walked in off the street, those who needed maybe a place to stay or a hot meal or some fresh clothes, or maybe just someone to talk to. During the week, several people in the church went to the parks to deliver sack lunches to the homeless. And once a week, they served a hot meal at the church, giving those who came a couple of bags of groceries for the week ahead.

Not everything that went on in that church was right. But the heart was right. And I think what was done there in Christ's name honored that name. What was done there was done with passion, both for God and for people. You could sense it in the way the people worshipped. You could see it in the way they went about helping those in need. Their lives, so much more than their words, touched me.

A Simple Mission Statement for Seminary

Here and there on my spiritual journey, other people have touched me like that. I think of Henri Nouwen, a remarkable man who had written some thirty books before he died. Most people know little, if anything, about him. He was a Catholic, which is one reason. He was not a radio or television personality, which is another. He was a priest who taught at Yale and Notre Dame and Harvard. He left the academic world to live among a community of mentally handicapped people. I think of his life, not his words, and thoughts of his life move me in profound ways, ways no sermon ever could, no seminar, no broadcast. His life haunts me in the most heavenly of ways, following me wherever I go, never letting me too far out of sight. His life haunts me the way Albert Schweitzer's life does, who went to Africa so his life rather than his words would be the sermon people would hear. Or the way Mother Teresa's life does, whose love for Jesus took her to India to serve Him there by serving the "the poorest of the poor."

Those three people were important to my spiritual formation. They heightened my awareness to the sacredness of the poor through whom Christ humbles Himself to come, almost like a sacrament. Those three people made me want to be more like them, which is to say, more like Christ, because it was Christ I saw so clearly and so compellingly in their lives.

They were important to my spiritual formation because in the seminary I attended the poor were not emphasized. Preaching was. That was the seminary's mission statement: "Preach the Word." A noble mission, certainly. And a necessary one. In case we have ever wondered how necessary, Paul's line of reasoning in Romans 10:13-14 should convince us. He starts by quoting a verse from the Old Testament. "Whoever will call upon the name of the Lord shall be saved." Then he traces the steps leading to that salvation: "How then shall they call upon Him in whom they have not believed? And how shall they believe in Him whom they have not heard? And how shall they hear without a preacher?"

Pretty sound logic. So is the logic of 1 Corinthians 13:1: "If I speak with the tongues of men and of angels, but do not have love, I have become a noisy gong or a clanging symbol." Paul is saying, essentially, that the mission statement for our lives needs to be broader than a task, no matter how biblical the task may be. Preach the Word. Reach the Lost. Equip the Saints. These are all part of God's mission for the body of Christ. But they are the hands and feet of that body, not its heart.

To reduce the body to the work it does is to diminish it. The body is so much more than that. The same is true of God. He is a lot of things. Omniscient is one of them. Infinite and immutable are two others. The list goes on and on. But in searching for one quality that captures the essence of who God is, would omniscience be the one we would pick? Or immutability? I don't think so. I think if we were to pick one statement that summarized who God is it would be the statement John picked: "God is love" (1 John 4:8). That is the heart of who He is. And what pulses through all His works (see Psalm 136).

When a mission statement focuses on what we do rather than who we are, its effects are far-reaching. Those effects can be seen in the way you and I schedule our day, in the way a church allocates its budget, in the way a seminary structures its curriculum.

When I was in seminary, the courses were structured to prepare us to exercise our gift, which for most of us there was teaching. The poor were only brought up when a passage we were studying spoke of them. I don't know what the seminary is like now, but at the time, a major in helping the poor wasn't offered. Not even a course. In the four years I spent there I never heard even a one-hour lecture on the subject, which is the second greatest commandment in the Bible we were being trained to preach.

So what happens after four years when we graduate? We preach, of course. And of course, we preach what we've been taught. And in the way we've been taught.

"What if" is a question writers are taught to ask their stories in order for the stories to develop, taking them to new and unexpected places the writers could not have imagined if they had not imagined "what if."

So, for a moment, let's imagine.

What if . . .

What if someone were to come to the seminary and empty the classrooms, get rid of everyone and start over with just the shell of a building?

What if, instead of a faculty drawn from the brightest academics, instead of a faculty with the right degrees from the right universities, instead of a faculty that was able to sign off on all the points and subpoints of a doctrinal statement, what if the only doctrinal statement they had to sign off on had only two points: Love the Lord your God with all your heart and soul and mind, and your neighbor as yourself?

What if it didn't matter whether they were Greek Orthodox or Amish, Baptist or Episcopalian, Charismatic or Evangelical, Protestant or Catholic? What if all that mattered were the passion of their love for God and for other people?

What if the mission statement were changed from "Preach the Word" to "Love the Lord your God with all your heart and soul and mind, and your neighbor as yourself"?

What difference would it make in the curriculum? What difference would it make in the students, not only in the type of students that applied but in the type of students that graduated?

What difference would it make in our churches?

In our world?

What difference would it make if all the meetings and activities that make up the curriculum of our lives were driven by that one, grand mission to passionately love God and allow that brimming love to slosh from our lives and drench everyone around us?

What difference would it make in what we pencil into our schedules?

In how we live our lives?

A Simple Mission Statement for Our Lives

The difference a person can make in your life, if that person really loves you, is extraordinary. I think of my grandmother, who loved like that. She was always fun to be around because she laughed a lot and teased a lot and you never got in her way, a fairly frequent thing kids get into when around adults. But not around this adult. Not with her grandkids, anyway. She rolled bandages for missionaries from strips of bedsheets, which is one of the things I remember when we visited her. When she visited us, which was once a year, she brought a bulging suitcase, complete with all her medications, which included Peppermint Schnapps, and of course "a little something" for each of us, candy or a coloring book or a little something she picked up somewhere and saved for one of her visists. She filled the house with the aroma of things she baked from scratch, and Canasta, which she taught us kids and brought us into the game around the table with the adults. She also filled the house with stories about Jesus. Invariably, one of those stories was about someone she met on the airplane on her way to visit us. Whenever she traveled, she always struck up conversations with whomever was seated next to her. And it didn't make any difference who it was, high school drop-out or corporate executive, her conversations always led to one question: "Do you love the Lord?" she would ask them. Not *know* Him, not *believe in* Him, but "Do you *love* Him?"

She of course asked me the very same question every time she visited. And of course I said yes, little knowing what all was involved in loving someone I couldn't hug or play Canasta with. I always said yes, I think as I reflect on it now, because I didn't want to disappoint her. I knew that loving the Lord was important to her, and since I loved her, that made it important to me. Not overnight, but over the years. Love has a way of rubbing off like that.

Who knows what spiritual energy lay dormant in that question she had planted in my young heart. Maybe something of that energy was what landed me in seminary. As I look back on my memories of her, she seemed to have the right emphasis, not only in the way she worded the question but in the way she lived her life. Though she is gone now, the way she lived her life lives with me still.

So does her question.

I never realized how much until I came across a quote by R.A. Torrey. I came across it long after I graduated from seminary, and, like my grandmother's question, I've never been able to get it out of my mind. Its simple yet powerful logic hit me like a punch to the chest. Here is the quote: "If loving God with all our heart and soul and might is the greatest commandment, then it follows that *not* loving him that way is the greatest sin."

Where can you hide from logic like that? What corner of your life can you run to for cover? Once you've heard it, how can you help from spending the rest of your life looking over your shoulder and listening for its footsteps? Because once you've heard it, it's going to follow you, maybe forever. *Hopefully* forever. Listen again as its hard soles echo off the sidewalks.

"If loving God with all our heart and soul and might is the greatest commandment, then it follows that *not* loving him that way is the greatest sin."

Of all the sins we talked about in seminary, and we talked about plenty, we never talked about that one. Never that one.

Sad, isn't it?

The only sadder thing is that it took me twenty years to wonder why.

Being a writer who only writes, who doesn't teach in a college or pastor a church, carries with it both a blessing and a curse. A curse, because it is often a lonely life filled with long hours of solitude. A blessing, for precisely the same reasons. My profession affords me large blocks of time with which to think, and for that I am thankful. As I've grown older, I've found a certain amount of anxiety creeps in to the thinking. You read cereal boxes, for example, not to find out what prize is inside but how much fiber. You start doing math with your food, trying to keep some kind of running total to know when you've hit your credit limit on fat calories. You start wondering [read "obsessing"] about little aches and pains you haven't noticed before, and thumbing through the family medical guide to see if your symptoms match some horrible, unpronounceable disease for which there is no cure known to man.

What I've been thinking about lately, and with a healthier sense of anxiety, is this. What constitutes a life that pleases God? The closer I get to the end of my life, it seems the only question that matters. Is the life I am living pleasing to God?

The question will keep you up nights. And it should. As we pull the covers to our chin and settle into our pillow, that's the question that should bring our day into the presence of God for His scrutiny. Did the life I lived today please you, God?

How many things do we have to check off on our to-do list before we can say yes to a question like that? How many questions do we have to count before we can be done with them all and drop off to sleep?

Only one.

Have I loved well?

When asked the secret of living the Christian life, Augustine replied: "Love God, and do as you please." The thought of that is both liberating and confining. Liberating because it means we are free to do whatever we want. Confining because it means our love for God sets the boundaries of that freedom. It guides every thought, every action, every conversation. And it does so every minute of the day, every day of our life. Instead of a Byzantine complexity of laws to regulate the details of our life, we have only one. The love of God. When that is the heart of who we are, it changes what we do. And it changes something else. How we will be judged.

St. John of the Cross once said that "at the evening of our day we shall be judged by our loving." As we look back over our day, *what* we have done is not as important as *how* we have done it. Better to do little with much love than much with little love. For without love, whatever we do will be dismissed with a judicial wave of heaven's hand as just so many trivial pursuits (1 Corinthians 13:1-3).

So it's the end of the day, and each of us is lying in our bed, reflecting. Have I loved well? Has love been the beating heart pulsing through all my activities? Can it be heard in all my conversations? Seen in my eyes? Felt when other people are in my presence? Was the truth I spoke today spoken in love? Were the decisions I made today based on love? Were my reactions? My devotions?

Have I loved well?

If we can answer yes to that question, it is enough.

It may not be enough for our employer. It may not be enough for our fellow workers. It may not be enough for all the carpools and committees and other things on our calendar.

It may not even be enough for us.

But it is enough for God.

And that should make it enough for us.

Habits of the Heart that Heighten Our Spiritual Senses

Reading without meditation is arid, meditation without reading is erroneous; prayer without meditation is tepid, meditation without prayer is fruitless.[1]

GUIGO

The Ladder of Monks

(12th-century manual of spiritual exercises)

Week after week we file into church where we nestle into our pews and dutifully go about the routines of the religious. We sing a few historic hymns, say one of the age-honored creeds, then settle back for the Sunday sermon.

If we're honest, we know we can almost do these things in our sleep. Sometimes we even do.

We hear the stalwart lyrics of a bygone era, but so often they seem to lose momentum with each century they traverse. We hear the robust statements of some Reformer's faith, but they seem so hollow, like faraway footsteps echoing off a cathedral floor. We hear the very words of God, but so often those words simply saunter around in our minds, kicking up nothing but a little intellectual dust.

Occasionally an impassioned imperative finds its way into our heart, but the soil upon which it falls is either so filled with competing loves or so overgrown with worry that seldom is there room for anything eternal to take root in our lives.

The same thing often happens with our personal devotions. We read our Bibles, fill in the blanks of our study guides, memorize our verses, all the while wondering. Why such slow growth? Why so little fruit? And why do the same old weeds keep cropping up, year after year?

Maybe some of the reason is due to the habits we have cultivated in our heart, or rather failed to cultivate, habits that nurture a more reflective way of living that opens our heart to catch those seeds.

The Three Habits

The three habits of the heart that nurture a reflective life are *reading the moment, reflecting on the moment,* and *responding to the moment.*

These habits can be applied to a passage of Scripture, a photograph, a person on the street, an advertisement in a magazine, a movie, something in nature, whatever we can see or hear or in some way experience.

The habits are simple:

Reading the moment is using our eyes to see what's on the surface.

Reflecting on the moment is engaging our mind to see what's beneath the surface.

Responding to the moment is giving what we have seen a place to live in our heart, allowing it to grow there, upward to God and outward to other people.

The Bible is full of people who cultivated these habits, sensitive not only to the Word of God but to what they saw of Him in nature, in history, and in the circumstances of their lives. Isaac reflected in a field in the early evening (Genesis 24:63). David reflected on his bed during the night (Psalm 63:6). Solomon reflected on a field during the day (Proverbs 24:30-32). The psalmists reflected on God's Law (Psalm 1:2), on nature (Psalm 19:3), on His wonders (Psalm 119:27), and on His attributes (Psalm 139:1-17). Mary reflected on the greeting spoken by the angel (Luke 1:29), on the story shared by the shepherds (2:19), and on the statement made by Jesus when He was twelve (2:51). Peter reflected on the perplexing image revealed to him in a vision (Acts 10:19). Paul reflected on incidents in Israel's history (1 Corinthians 10:1-11). And the entire Book of Hebrews is essentially reflections on the meaning behind Old Testament symbols and practices.

The Three Habits Applied to Studying the Moments of God's Word

There is a long and almost unbroken tradition in Church history of believers reading the Word of God, reflecting on it, and using their reflections as the starting point for prayerfully responding. This is the natural process of assimilating God's Word. To read the Word without reflecting on it is like sitting at a table where a sumptuous meal has been prepared and eyeing all the food but never eating. To reflect on the Word without prayerfully responding is like chewing the food but never swallowing. The way we are nourished spiritually is similar to the way we are nourished physically. First we sit at the table and cut off a bite of food, then we chew it, then we swallow it so that bite by bite the meal can be digested and assimilated. That is not only the natural process for our spiritual nourishment, it is the essential process.

The benefits of reflecting on the Scriptures is highlighted in the Psalms (19:7-11, 119:11, 97-100), especially in Psalm 1.

How blessed is the man who does not walk in the counsel of the wicked,
Nor stand in the path of sinners,
Nor sit in the seat of scoffers!
But his delight is in the law of the Lord,
And in His law he meditates day and night.
And he will be like a tree firmly planted by streams of water,
Which yields its fruit in its season,
And its leaf does not wither;
And in whatever he does, he prospers. (vv. 1-3)

The Hebrew word for *meditate* means "to mutter or to mumble, to make a low sound." It is used of the gentle cooing of a dove, the low growl of a lion, and the soft music of a harp. It was the habit of people reflecting on the Scriptures to turn the words over and over in their mind, and they did this by speaking the words, often in a whisper that sounded very much like mumbling. They would do this on an early-morning walk, on a garden bench in the afternoon, or on their bed at night. Going over and over the words worked something like a root stimulator, allowing the words to penetrate their heart more quickly and more deeply.

This process of reflection was not a rote exercise. Notice in verse 2 the word that stands in parallel to *meditate*. It is *delight.* The pairing of these two words reveals that both the heart and the mind are essential in the process of reflection. Like sap and the woody fiber of a tree. Sap without the fiber results in formless life. Fiber without the sap results in lifeless form.

"Delight" is a dominate theme of Psalm 119, which is not only the longest chapter in the Bible but one that speaks almost exclusively about God's Word (vv. 16, 24, 35, 47, 70, 77, 92, 143, 174). Like the word *meditate*, it has an interesting meaning. It means "excited attention." The Word of God is not simply one of many subjects of study for this man, it is his *favorite* subject. It keeps him up at night (Psalm 63:6). It keeps him company when he wakes up in the morning (Psalm 139:18).

He delights in it the way someone delights in handling pure gold or in tasting rich honey (Psalm 19:7-11). The word is used in 1 Kings 10:13, where Solomon has escorted the Queen of Sheba around his court, showing her all his riches, his battalions of gold shields, a throne of ivory overlaid with gold, drinking vessels of pure gold, precious stones, exotic animals, the best of food, an endless entourage of servants, all finely attired, and a sweeping stairway that led to the house of the Lord. It was all so breathtaking that when the Queen saw it, the text says "there was no more spirit in her" (v. 5).

Once she catches her breath, she tells him, "It was a true report which I heard in my own land about your words and your wisdom. Nevertheless I did not believe the reports, until I came and my eyes had seen it. And behold, the half was not told me. You exceed in wisdom and prosperity the report which I heard" (vv. 6-7). What Solomon does next is let her take a shopping cart through the palace and take whatever excited her attention. He gave the Queen whatever was her "desire" (v. 13), the word *desire* being the same word in Psalm 1, translated *delight*.

The person who approaches the Word of God in this way is pictured as a tree. But not simply a tree. A tree planted by and overhanging the "streams of water." This phrase is a technical term, meaning "water canals." The use of the term here indicates that the picture we are looking at is not of a tree that grows beside a river, which may flood or recede according to the weather. It is a tree growing in a garden. The eastern garden back then was usually walled (Proverbs 24:31, Isaiah 5:5) and crisscrossed with irrigation ditches. The trees in that garden grew under the care of a gardener who watched over it and controlled the flow of water into it (Deuteronomy 11:10).

In such a well-cultivated and well-protected spot, the tree flourished. The picture is one of stability, security, beauty, vitality, and productivity. This description of a tree stands at the introduction to the Book of Psalms almost like a frontispiece etching with an onion skin overlay in some leather-bound, gilt-edged classic. Its themes branch throughout the book, reaching full leaf in Psalm 119, which pictures the fruit of reflecting on God's Word, hanging heavy on the limb.

(For additional thoughts on the subject, see Appendix A, where there are sample selections from the devotional book, *Reflections on the Word*.)

The Three Habits Applied to Journaling the Moments of Our Day

In a journal entry dated August 5, 1851, Henry David Thoreau wrote: "The question is not what you look at, but what you see."[2]

That is one of the benefits of keeping a journal. It helps us see what we look at. When we journal, it's like taking a Polaroid of some moment during the day that has caught our attention. Only we do it with words instead of with film. But like that film, what we have looked at often develops right before our very eyes as we're writing, revealing things we hadn't seen before.

My reflections on the everyday moments of my life are, for the most part, a hodgepodge. Some have actually found their way into journals. Others lie pressed between sheaves of inconsequential things I've boxed away over the years. Others mark places in books. Still others are unaccounted for. I know I wrote them down . . . somewhere . . . I just can't remember where.

What is important about our reflections is not so much that they find their way into a journal but that they find their way into our heart. Of course, if we can't find our reflections, they're likely to get lost along the way. Which is why a journal is helpful. And why some form of order in the journal is helpful, too, whether that order is chronological or topical. Mine, for the most part, are chronologically arranged, more sporadic and random, with something different on every page.

On one page, for example, is a list of the books I've read that year, along with the movies I've seen. I do this as a way of marking the trail, so to speak, to remember where I've been on my spiritual pilgrimage and what has touched me along the way.

On another page is a movie review of *Shoah*, a Holocaust documentary I saw, which I clipped from the newspaper and taped into my journal so I wouldn't forget it.

On one page are quotes I've gathered. This one, by the Scottish writer George MacDonald, was particularly rich for reflection:

Nor will God force any door to enter in. He may send a tempest about the house; the wind of His admonishment may burst doors and windows, yea, shake the house to its foundations; but not then, not so, will He enter. The door must be opened by the willing hand, ere the foot of Love will cross the threshold. He watches to see the door move from within. Every tempest is but an assault in the seige of Love. The terror of God is but the other side of His love; it is love outside, that would be inside—love that knows the house is no house, only a place, until it enter.

On another page of the journal is me whining about my life, which I will mercifully spare you.

On another page is a letter from a friend: "Dear Ken—My friend Tim died on Wednesday, February 24 of complications from AIDS. . . ."

On another page I taped a drawing of Tim by our daughter, Kelly, along with her thoughts.

On the next page is a drawing of Tim by our oldest daughter, Gretchen, along with some of her thoughts: "Last night a friend of ours died. He had been in a Broadway play. . . . His name was Tim. He spent Christmas with us. He taught me some neat dance steps. I really liked him. He was a very gentle and kind person."

On another page are some reflections I had written after a Thanksgiving meal Judy had prepared in remembrance of Tim.

Journaling is a gathering of moments like these that opens a dialogue with God about life. And not just about life in general but about our life in particular. In this case, it opened for me a dialogue with God about the death of a friend, and how to tell my kids. About AIDS. And homosexuality.

My reflections led to questions. How would Jesus have responded to

Tim? What would He have said in a phone call? What would He have written in a letter? Would He have loved the man who had fallen among thieves? If so, would He have touched him . . . carried him over His shoulder . . . cleansed his wounds . . . cared for him?

Certainly He would have. Of course. How could we have ever thought otherwise?

Yet sometimes it takes writing those questions down in a journal before we discover the answer to those questions and what God would have us do to show love to the neighbor dying on the roadside.

A journal, to use Thoreau's words, helps us to see what we look at. To see beneath the surface of a person's life. To see, for example, that beneath Tim's sexuality was his humanity. To see that there is more to a woman than the fact that she is some man's wife, more to her even than her own femaleness. That there is more to a Republican than his politics. And more to a Democrat, too.

There is more to us than what people see.

We see a lot of things we haven't seen in people when we're given a peek into their journal. There we see them with their make-up off and their mat of morning hair. And seeing them like that helps us not only to understand them better but to love them better. But the journals of most people are mostly private. Every once in a while, though, someone's journal is published and we see them in ways we maybe never imagined.

You get to know people more through their journal, I think, than through anything else they have written. In a book someone has written, for example, everything is rewritten and edited and proofread. I remember reading *The Grapes of Wrath* by John Steinbeck and admiring not only the craftsmanship of his prose but his insights into the human condition. Steinbeck was a Nobel Prize-winning author so he *should be* insightful, he *should be* confident in his craft.

What he should be, though, was so different from what he was. I saw beneath the polish of his prose one day when I was browsing the shelves of a used bookstore. It was his familiar name on the spine of an unfamiliar book that caught my eye. The book was titled, *Working Days*, and it was the journal he kept during the writing of *The Grapes of Wrath*. Reading it, I learned that the title of the novel came from his wife, who thought the line from the Civil War hymn captured the story's essence. The research, I learned, was not mostly from firsthand observation but secondhand, from a man who had studied migrant workers, following them from camp to camp, listening to what they talked about, how they expressed themselves, what figures of speech they used. And Steinbeck, I learned, was anything but confident in his abilities. He was full of self-doubt, worried at how slow the writing was going, wondering if he would be able to meet his deadline, and if what he had written was any good. And he was crabby about all the distracting noise his neighbor's remodeling project was making. All this to say, the more accurate picture of Steinbeck was captured in the journal, not the novel.

When I look back on my own journals, especially the ones I kept during my formative years as a writer, I always see something I haven't seen before. All of those daily entries form a composite of who I once was and who I was in the process of becoming. It looks to me less like an author's photo on the book jacket and more like a wanted poster in the post office. The picture is full of insecurities, anxieties, introspections, shortsightedness, and pendulum swings of optimism and pessimism. That is who I was back then. It is also something of who I am even now.

Journaling is what preserved that picture. The Holy Spirit is who helped me to see it. I couldn't see those things then. Now they're obvious. When I recorded those moments, I could do little more with them than a surface reading. Only after years could I gain anything from reflecting on them. And only after reflecting on them did I have anything to respond to.

That is why the journal is important. Not as a scrapbook, to chronicle our lives, but as a way of reflecting on our lives so we can better understand who we were and where we've been . . . better understand where we are going and what it is that is driving us there . . . better understand how we should change if where we are being driven is destructive to us and to those around us.

And so the journal becomes a way not only to understand ourselves better, but to love ourselves better. The way God loves us. The way He would have us to love ourselves and to care for ourselves, the way the Good Samaritan cared for the man who had fallen among thieves.

To better love others and to better love ourselves is reason enough to keep a journal. But there is a more important reason.

The most important reason for keeping a journal is that every now and then God shows up. Reading the moments of our day helps us to see Him when He does. Reflecting on those moments helps us to hear what He is saying. Responding to those moments is a way of losing our life so we can find the life He wants us to have. When we live like that, the moments of our days become a confession of faith, that God is our master and we are His servants put here to do His will.

Some of that will is revealed in the Scriptures.

Some is revealed in the circumstances of our lives.

Journaling helps us to discern what God may be saying to us through those circumstances. For God loves us so much that He sent His Son, the very Word of God, not only to die for us but to live for us, not only to be with us to the end of the age but to speak with us along the way.

(For additional thoughts on journaling, see Appendix B, where there are sample selections from the journal, *Reflections on Your Life.*)

The Three Habits Applied to Scheduling the Moments of Our Lives

Today, more than any time in history, the plates set before us are filled with all sorts of good things. Planes, boats, trains, and cars to take us anywhere we want to go, even off-road, with radios and reading material to keep the ride from ever getting boring. We have sports to make our lives more fun. Clothes to make our lives more attractive. Hobbies to make our lives more interesting. Television, movies, and the theater to make our lives more entertaining. Books, magazines, and newspapers to make our lives more informed. Tools, electronic gadgets, and computers to make our lives more efficient. Vacations to make our lives more relaxed. Educational opportunities to make our lives deeper. Social events, small-group meetings, and church to make our lives richer. Volunteer opportunites to make our lives more meaningful.

So with all those things filling our lives, why aren't we more fulfilled?

Maybe it has something to do with the fact that life is like an all-you-can-eat buffet, which looks good as we're going through the serving line, but by the time we're finished eating, everything has lost its taste. And instead of feeling satisfied, we feel bloated.

Sometimes less is more, as the saying goes, and sometimes a few well-prepared servings are more satisfying, ones where we have time to chew, where we can taste even the subtlest of spices, where the flavor lingers long after we've finished.

We can't savor anything, though, if we're stuffed. And if we're heaping serving after serving onto our schedule, by the end of the day we're never going to want to eat again.

Putting pauses into our schedule allows us to savor the individual servings in our day. Let me change metaphors from eating to reading, and I'll try to say what I mean in another way.

The following is a chapter from my book, *Windows of the Soul*. The chapter is about pausing and covers eleven pages. In an attempt to get as many words on the fewest pages, I have reduced the type and taken out all the spaces I could, from those between paragraphs to those between pages. Take a few minutes and read it.

PAUSING AT THE WINDOWThe problem is not entirely in finding the room of one's own, the time alone, difficult and necessary as that is. The problem is more how to still the soul in the midst of its activities.Anne Morrow LindberghGift from the SeaWindows of the soul offer glimpses, however fleeting, and echoes, however faint, of some of the things that are dear to God.I caught one of those glimpses on a Sunday afternoon obscured with activity.It should have been a day to push back the papers that cluttered the desk of my soul, but the papers were urgent and I was anxious I was behind on a writing project with a fast-approaching deadline, so I had set aside Sunday afternoon to spend catching up.Early that afternoon, though, my daughter asked if I would take her to see a friend who was playing in a roller hockey game. The friend was a boy whom I'll call Joey. He had cerebral palsy, my daughter said, and he had asked her at school Friday if she would come and watch him play. She told him she would, if she could get a ride.As it turned out, I was the only ride available.I said yes, knowing if I didn't, that something precious would be lost, and though I didn't know what that was, I knew it was greater than whatever could be gained by saying no.When we arrived at the roller rink, I went in with her, thinking I could find a quiet nook and get some work done. But inside all kinds of noises echoed off the bare walls and slatted wood floor. Video arcades lined one of the walls, luring young boys with lose change. A concession stand lined another, luring the rest of us. Families of the players milled around, talking; several of them leaning against the perimeter railing.I was looking for an out-of-the way place to write when my daughter pointed out Joey. He was playing goalie, hidden behind shin guards, face mask, and a chest guard. He had been positioned where he didn't have to move much, so I hardly noticed he was handicapped. All I noticed was that he stood a foot taller and years older than the other players.Gathered at the railing behind Joey were four boys from my daughter's school. She joined them while I nested in a vacant table, taking out my pen and notebook, busying myself with all the catching up I had scheduled for that afternoon. But the sight of those five high school kids and the sound of their cheering distracted me. I stopped and paused and wondered if there was something I should be paying attention to, something that might prove to be a window of the soul.I turned to a fresh page.I watched. I listened. And I framed the moment with words."Way to go, Joey," one of the boys calls out.The other team scores against him."It's alright, Joey."Joey blocks a shot.The five high school kids cheer. "Way to go, Joey."The game goes back and forth from the far goal to the near one. Joey shows dissatisfaction with the way he's playing."Don't worry, Joey."The four boys sit clumped on a round table. My daughter is off to the side. Joey makes another save, and all of them cheer. My daughter finally gets tired of standing and sits on the table with the boys."Way to hustle. Great defense. Yeah.""Good job, Joey."One by one they get up and lean on the railing, closer to the action. Joey pounds the floor with his hockey stick."Joey, you're doing great."In a letter dated October 10, 1907, the poet Rilke talks about his first exposure to the artwork of Cezanne, how he spent hours in front of his pictures, looking, listening, trying to understand them: "I remember the puzzlement and insecurity of one's first confrontation with his work, along with his name, which is just as new. And then for a long time nothing, and suddenly one has the right eyes."I sat in front of the picture, looking, listening, trying to understand it. For a long time nothing. Then a memory of the widow at the Temple made a silhouette of my thoughts. She was a person no one noticed until Jesus framed her with his words. I thought of the picture of that poor widow. And of the passage where Jesus talks about giving to the poor. Then of Joey. And suddenly I have the right eyes. Suddenly I realized that there are many ways a person can be impoverished, and sometimes the least of those ways is materially. That was the case with Joey. His poverty was not material; it was relational. He didn't need money or what money could buy. He needed something it couldn't buy---friends. He needed, as we all need, friends who will talk to him in the hall and sit with him at lunch and have him over to spend the night. He needed, as we all need, friends who will show up at a cross-town roller rink, lean against the railing, and cheer him on. Some people are rich in friends like that. Joey isn't.Joey is an impoverished kid groping for his soul's daily bread in the halls of his high school. With sometimes lame and socially awkward overtures, he accosts his classmates, holding out his hand for a crust of what they have in such abundance. He begs them to look beyond the disease and all it has robbed him of. He begs them to look beyond the slur of his words and the shuffle of his feet. He begs them to see Joey. Of course, he can't put it into words like that or into any words close to that. His inarticulate emotions can express themselves only in frustration, bouts of depression, and outbursts of anger. It's the way of the artist, calling to those walking away from his art, begging they come back and look beyond the paint to see the passion of his soul enflamed on the canvas.With the language of emotion, a complex and sometimes indecipherable language, Joey is begging us to look beyond the jarring anddisjointed Picasso that his life appears to be on the surface, pleading with us to see within him the beautiful and breathtaking Michelangelo, which is no less than the very image of God. "If we are to love our neighbors," says Frederick Buechner, "before doing anything else we must see our neighbors. With our imagination as well as with our eyes, that is to say like artists, we must see not just their faces but the life behind and within their faces."That day I saw something behind the face of the hockey mask and behind the face of cerebral palsy. I saw Joey.Besides Joey, I wondered what else there was to see in that roller rink on that Sunday afternoon. I looked beyond him to the five kids still at the railing. They could have been at the video arcade. They could have been at the concession stand. They could have been at the table, talking among themselves, joking among themselves, preoccupied with themselves. And who could blame them if they were? We would be there ourselves, doing the same things ourselves, wouldn't we?But they weren't there; they were at the railing. They weren't preoccupied with themselves; they were preoccupied with Joey. Watching him. Encouraging him. Cheering him on.And as they did, something changed hands. What was it? I squinted. A gift of some sort. A gift Joey desperately needed. Neither the hands of the giver nor the hands of the receiver were aware of the exchange. But the Father who sees in secret, He saw it, He took note of it, He treasured it. And so did I.Was that all there was to see in that picture? Or was there more?I looked again. For a long time nothing. And suddenly again I have the right eyes. Beyond Joey and beyond the gift that had been given him, I saw a girl who had given up her Sunday afternoon to help give that gift. She could have asked to be there. She could have asked to be somewhere else, the mall, the movies, anywhere. But she asked to be there. She told a boy with cerebral palsy she would watch him play if she could find a ride. She found a ride. And she kept a promise to someone for whom promises were not so much broken as they were simply forgotten. The picture was a window to my daughter's soul, revealing to me something of the secret of who she is, a secret I will need to know if I am to understand her and nurture her and draw out in her all that is dear to God.That Sunday afternoon in that roller rink I saw something sacred, something dear to God. And in a sudden, somewhat sobering moment, I realized I was the only person on earth who had seen it. Something about that made me feel special, excited to be alive at just that place and at just that time to see then and there what no one else had seen.And yet something about being the only one also made me feel sad. The moment did something to me that I can't quiet put my finger on, let alone, find words for. Maybe there are no words for such moments in a person's life. Maybe some moments are too sacred for words. What I experienced that day was profoundly moving, and one of the places it moved me was to wonder: How many windows have I missed because I was too busy to look? And how much wisdom have I overlooked because I was too behind in my schedule to even see what was being offered?The problem is not entirely in finding a quiet nook in this roller rink world of ours. The problem is quieting the soul in the midst of the noise.But quieting the soul of a writer, who once fed a family of six from odd jobs and sometimes no jobs at all, is no small task. In those days I spent most of my time waiting for better times. I waited for the day the book would get written, and for the day it would get sent off. I waited for the day the publisher would reply, which was most of the time a form-letter and all of the time a letter of rejection. I waited for the day when something I wrote would get published. When that day finally came, I continued to wait, partly because by now I was really good at it, and partly at least because I was at a time in my life when I needed to feel I was good at something, even at such a small thing as waiting. So I waited for the first copy to come from the printer, and when I got it, I waited for the first copies to arrive at the bookstores. After that I waited for the first royalty check to come, to see if I had a career or just lunch money for the next week.I lived a book at a time, a check at a time, and charted the course for my future, for all six of our futures, from a sextant fixed on just such dim starlight as that.Someday I would write. Someday I would get something published. Someday I would be a full-time writer, making a living at what I loved. But while I was living for all those somedays, I was missing all my todays. I was so busy getting where I wanted to be I forgot where I was and what was being offered me there by the generous hand of God.Seeing windows in my day-to-day life changed all that, quieting the noise in my soul as I began to realize not only what was being offered, but by whom. And as I began to receive what was offered, not someday but today.Today, though, has its own whirl of responsibilities, and if we get caught up in the spin, the windows of the soul will blur by us. To keep that from happening, Anne Morrow Lindbergh suggests we strive "to be the still axis within the revolving wheel of relationships, obligations, and activities." The still axis.It is able to maintain its center no matter how fast the wheel is turning. It is, in fact, what keeps the wheel turning. Without the axis being still, the wheel would wobble off or else bind up and bring everything lurching to a stop. Stillness is what gives stability. And it is what keeps the wheels from falling off our lives.The problem is not indigenous to our times, however fast-paced and frenetic those times may seem. The problem is as old as humanity and as ingrained as human nature. Paging back two thousand years and peering through the window of another culture, we see the same problem in the home of two sisters. One is a still axis; the other is caught in a revolving wheel.As Jesus and his disciples were on their way, he came to a village where a woman named Martha opened her home to him. She had a sister called Mary, who sat at the Lord's feet listening to what he said. But Martha was distracted by all the preparations that had to be made. She came to him and asked, "Lord, don't you care that my sister has left me to do the work by myself? Tell her to help me!""Martha, Martha," the Lord answered, "you are worried and upset about many things, but only one thing is needed. Mary has chosen what is better, and it will not be taken away from her." (Luke 10:38--42)What do we see at that window? The disciples are with Jesus initially, but they don't appear to be with him now. Why? Is the house too small? Do they all need a break from each other after being on the road for so long? Is Jesus tired, is that why he comes to this house? Is he hungry? If so, for what? For food? Or is he hungry for something else, something that maybe the crowds and his disciples can't give him?Jesus is on the way to Jerusalem, on the way to his death. A few miles before he gets there, he stops here, at the home of these two women. He stops here, I think, because he is hungry for someone who will listen, someone who will understand, someone who will feel something of the heaviness he carries with him on that uphill road to Jerusalem. Yes, he is hungry. But not for food.Which of these hungers does Martha see when she greets him at the door? Does she see a window into what is going on inside him, a window into what he is thinking, feeling, needing? Or does she see just the leanness in his face and the angle of the sun, telling her it's nearly time for dinner? Martha goes to the kitchen to prepare that dinner, leaving Mary sitting at Jesus' feet. What words is he aching to say, not just to Mary but to both of them? What words is he aching to hear, not just from Mary but from both of them?Only one of them, though, pauses at that window. Only one of them sees the hunger in his soul. And it's not Martha. Martha's in the kitchen. She works faster to make up for Mary's absence, but the faster she works the more steamed-up she gets. Finally she wipes the sweat from her face and storms out of the kitchen with a frying-pan-of-a-question waving in her hand. But why does she shake it at Jesus and not at Mary? And why does she refer to her as "my sister" instead of by name? The answers to those questions reveal something not only of her frustration but her anger. Can you hear in her question not just the irritation but the indictment? "Lord, don't you care?" Instead of waiting for an answer, Martha issues an order. What does that tell you about the nature of her question and about the tone of voice she used in asking it? But her wrath is met with a gentle answer. There is great tenderness in Jesus' reply. Can you hear it? In the past I have more or less identified with Mary. But over the years, as I have had the opportunity to look deeper into my life, the more I see of Martha. The truth, I think, is that there is something of both sisters in all of us. And that is why so many of us so much of the time find ourselves in the middle of an inner tug-of-war, pulled one way by our duties and another by our devotion. The words spoken to Martha are words spoken also to the Martha in me. But what were those words correcting? It was her worry, not her work. It was her being upset, not her being under pressure. The issue wasn't her preparations; it was her distractions. It wasn't the many things; it was that the many things didn't revolve around the one thing that was needed. There was no quiet center that Martha was working from, no solitude of heart, no still axis around which her activities revolved. That's why the wheels fell off her attitude. And that's why, with some regularity, they fall off of mine. When my attitude starts to wobble, I know it's because I'm distracted. I don't realize how much I'm distracted, though, until the axis starts grinding and heating up. Like Martha, I get frustrated, irritated, and sometimes stomping-mad-tell-somebody-off angry. I know a wheel is starting to fall off when the meal I'm preparing becomes more important than the people I'm preparing it for. When my work becomes more important than the family I'm working for. When a point I'm making becomes more important than the person I'm making it to. That's how I can I tell I've lost the still axis. When I lose sight of what's more important. When I lose a sense of the sacredness of another human being, especially the human beings closest to me, the ones in my family. I want to live in a way so that I don't lose sight of what's important or lose a sense of the sacredness of others. I want to live in a way so I can see windows of the soul. I don't want to live in the kitchen of religious activity, distracted with all my preparations. I don't want to live slumped over some steamed-up stove, worried and upset about so many things. I want to live at the Savior's feet, gazing into his eyes, listening to his words, and seeing as many windows as he'll show me. At his feet is where we learn to pause at those windows. It starts by loving him and longing to hear his voice. When we're slaving away in some kitchen where the pots and pans are clanging, it's hard to hear that voice. But when we're at his feet and our heart is still, we can hear him even when he whispers. A Prayer for Solitude Help me, O God, To be a still axis in the wheel of activities that revolves around my life. Deliver me from my distractions, which are many, and lead me to a quiet place of devotion at your feet. Teach me there how to pause at more windows. I know I won't see everything, but help me see something. So much passes me by without attention, let alone, appreciation; without reflection, let alone, reverence; without thought, let alone, thankfulness. Slow me down, Lord, so I may see the windows in roller rinks and the overarching grandeur of your image in the Sistine Chapel of the soul...[3]

At what point did you stop reading?

A third of the way through? Halfway through?

At what point did you stop reflecting on what you had read? Did you even start?

If you stopped reading and didn't pause or reflect, how could your heart have had a chance to respond to what was written, to be touched by it in some way, or softened by it, even broken by it?

The pauses give resonance to the words, giving them a place to live in our heart. That is why it's important to schedule pauses into our day. The pauses give resonance to the words we read, whether those words are spoken through a Scripture that comes to mind or through a billboard that blurs by us on the freeway or through a boy at the roller rink (he's in the first half of the chapter on pausing, if you missed him).

A busy schedule crowds out those pauses. When life pressures us to put as much as we can into a day, we start reducing the type, combining paragraphs, editing out the spaces, eliminating the margins.

And after a while, we simply stop reading.

PART VI

The Growth of the Reflective Life

A man's mind may be likened to a garden, which may be intelligently cultivated or allowed to run wild; but whether cultivated or neglected, it must, and will, *bring forth*.[1]

JAMES ALLEN

As a Man Thinketh

Reflecting on the Scriptures

My suggestion is that you take a single event, or a parable, or a few verses, or even a single word and allow it to take root in you. Seek to live the experience, remembering the encouragement of Ignatius of Loyola to apply all our senses to our task. Smell the sea. Hear the lap of water along the shore. See the crowd. Feel the sun on your head and the hunger in your stomach. Taste the salt in the air. Touch the hem of his garment. In this regard Alexander Whyte counsels us, ". . . the truly Christian imagination never lets Jesus Christ out of her sight. . . . You open your New Testament. . . . And, by your imagination, that moment you are one of Christ's disciples on the spot, and are at his feet."[1]

R I C H A R D   F O S T E R

Celebration of Discipline

I n this section I would like to walk you through some applications of the three habits of the heart that I discussed in the previous section. Although the three habits can be applied to every area of life, here we will apply them to only three: the Scriptures, other people, and the arts, with the arts being divided into the movies and the theater. The first area we will examine will be the Scriptures.

When I wrote several devotional books of vignettes on the life of Christ, I attempted to do what Alexander Whyte suggested—to place the reader for a moment at the Savior's feet.

But before I could place the reader there, I had to place myself there first. Here's how I did that. I tried to visualize the passage, looking at it the way I would a scene from a movie, using textual clues to recreate the atmosphere.

I would, to use Richard Foster's words, try to "smell the sea. Hear the lap of water along the shore. See the crowd. Feel the sun on your head and the hunger in your stomach. Taste the salt in the air. Touch the hem of his garment."

To walk you through the process, here are the steps I more or less went through in my reflections that led to one of the moments in my *Moments with the Savior* books. Although the steps can be grouped under the longer strides of reading, reflecting, and responding, for the purposes of this exercise I have broken them down into smaller units.

Reading the Moment

Frame the Passage

The first step I take is to isolate the passage. In the passage I have chosen for consideration, Luke 10:38-42 frames the scene.

> Now as they were traveling along, He entered a certain village; and a woman named Martha welcomed Him into her home. And she had a sister called Mary, who moreover was listening to the Lord's word, seated at His feet.
>
> But Martha was distracted with all her preparations; and she came up to Him, and said, "Lord, do You not care that my sister has left me

to do all the serving alone? Then tell her to help me."

But the Lord answered and said to her, "Martha, Martha, you are worried and bothered about so many things; but only a few things are necessary, really only one, for Mary has chosen the good part, which shall not be taken away from her."

Place the Passage in Its Proper Context

After I frame the text, I look for the context. Most often the context can be discovered by looking at the verses before and after the passage in question. In this case, the verses following the passage don't shed much light on the context. Neither do the verses before it. The *chapter* before it, however, does. In the previous chapter in Luke we are told that "It came about, when the days were approaching for His ascension, that He resolutely set His face to go to Jerusalem" (9:51). From that verse we learn two things. That Jesus was aware His appointment with death was approaching. And, that He was resolved to meet that appointment. This means, of course, that He had given up hope of Israel receiving Him as the Messiah. Reading further, we discover that Jesus had just crossed the hot and unreceptive deserts of Samaria (vv. 52-56). Both passages hint at the emotions that must have been churning within Jesus before He arrived at Mary's and Martha's house.

Cross-reference the Passage

Cross-referencing a passage is a good way to give dimension to the scene. There are several ways to do this. Looking up key words in a concordance is the best way. Another way is to look in the margin of your Bible, where a shorter, more select list of references is sometimes placed. The marginal reading in the *New American Standard Bible* of Luke 10:38 points to several such references. Looking up one of them, John 11:1, we learn the identity of the "certain village" where Jesus stopped. "Now a certain man was sick, Lazarus of Bethany, the village of Mary and her sister Martha.

As we read through John 11, the passage where Jesus raised Lazarus, we discover something crucial to our understanding of the Mary and Martha passage. Verse five states: "Now Jesus loved Martha, and her sister, and Lazarus." Knowing that, we realize that the home of Mary and Martha was an oasis of rest between the geographical desert that lay behind Jesus and the spiritual desert that lay before him. How Jesus must have looked forward to coming there.

By looking up Mary's name in a concordance and sifting through the references, we see that this particular Mary is mentioned only three times in the Bible (Luke 10:39, John 11:32, 12:3). Each of those times she is at the Savior's feet, which reveals something about her and about her relationship with Jesus. Her physical posture reflects her spiritual posture, for to put yourself at another's feet is an act of humility, acknowledging the other person's superiority and, at the same time, your subservience.

Detail the Passage

If we want to find details about the village of Bethany, there are a few places we can look. A Bible atlas and a Bible dictionary are two of them. Consulting an atlas, we discover that Bethany is a small town only a couple of miles outside of Jerusalem. It is not a big, bustling city like Jerusalem. It is more like a quiet suburb.

Reflecting on the Moment

Question the Passage

Now that the lines of the scene are clearly in focus, we're in a position to ask some questions that can fill in some of the color. This is where the shift takes place between reading and reflection. I try to place myself in the scene, one moment looking through Christ's eyes, then Martha's eyes, then Mary's.

I try to imagine what Jesus must have felt, knowing the clock was ticking down to the hour of His death. I imagine what last words He would want to say, and to whom He would want to say them, and how He would hope those words would be received. Reflecting like that helps to move us from the surface of a scene to its heart.

When Jesus showed up at Martha's home, what did she see standing before her in the doorway? Did she see a man with sorrow in His eyes? Did she sense the heaviness in His heart? No. What she saw was an unexpected guest who needed feeding. How do we know that? In the opening scene we see her welcoming Jesus into the home, but we don't see her again until she comes out of the kitchen. Had she taken the time to sit with Jesus, as Mary had done, she would have discovered that, though He was hungry, it wasn't for food. It was for fellowship. The rejection that lay behind Him in Samaria and the crucifixion that awaited Him in Jerusalem undoubtedly troubled Him. He was weary from carrying these things inside Him and was looking for a place where He could lay his burdens down. Jesus had things He wanted to say to someone who cared, someone who understood, someone who would listen. He tried to tell His disciples, but anytime He mentioned His death, they didn't know what to make of it.

He found that someone who cared, who understood, who would listen, in Mary. She sat at His feet, listening to His words, easing His burdens by taking them into her heart, shouldering something of His rejection, His sadness, His grief.

Martha, meanwhile, was busy in the kitchen where she was not only whipping up a meal but working up an attitude. How do we know that? Look at the text.

> She came up to Him, and said, "Lord, do You not care that my sister has left me to do all the serving alone?"

Martha went to Jesus with her grievance instead of to Mary. What does that tell you about her attitude? How upset was she with Mary? What does it tell you about her level of irritation that she refers to Mary as "my sister" instead of by name? Read the verse again, this time listening to how Martha worded her question and see if you can pick up the tone of her voice. What does her question reveal about the thoughts she must have been having in the kitchen? The fact that Martha accused Jesus of not caring shows that her anger toward Mary had spilled onto Him. Listen to what follows.

> "Then tell her to help me."

Did Martha wait for an answer to her question? No. What does that tell you about her reason for asking it? Did she ask for an explanation? No, she was merely venting her anger.

By reading the verses carefully and reflecting upon them, the sound and color of the original scene are restored. So is the emotion. Which heightens the contrast between Martha's words to Jesus and His words to her.

"Martha, Martha, you are worried and bothered about so many things."

Notice how easily the "many things" in Martha's life caused her not only to be distracted but irritated, how even something as mundane as meal preparation worried her and bothered her, affecting not only her relationship with her sister but with Christ.

In contrast to life's many responsibilities, Jesus says that only a few things are really necessary. And, when you get right down to it, only one. The one thing necessary, the one thing of eternal value, the one thing that shall not be taken away, is the time we spend seated at Christ's feet, looking into His eyes with adoration and listening to His word in submission.

Do Word Studies on the Passage

Sometimes a passage of Scripture contains a key word or phrase that helps elucidate the text. Often the word in question will be self-evident because the text draws attention to it. In this case, the Lord Himself drew attention to it. It is "the good part."

What exactly *is* the good part? We can pretty much figure that out from the context. It is fellowship with Christ. But when we look up this word, either in a commentary or a Greek lexicon, another layer of meaning comes to light. The term *part* is often used of a portion of food and was used here by Jesus as a word play to contrast the nourishment He offered with the food that Martha had been preparing. The best part of the meal, Jesus told Martha, wasn't in the kitchen. It was being served at the place where Mary was sitting.

Make the Language Contemporary When Possible

Sometimes it helps to do a little imaginative translation with certain words or phrases in order to understand them more fully. To see how the word play would translate into today's language, for example, imagine a sumptuous Thanksgiving meal with all the trimmings. Hillocks of mashed potatoes and dressing, sluiced with gravy, hot buttered rolls, cranberry sauce, an assortment of salads, trays of deviled eggs, olives, sweet pickles, slabs of pumpkin pie daubed with homemade whipped cream. All those things look wonderful, smell wonderful, taste wonderful.

Now imagine that meal without the turkey.

The portion around which all the other food is centered is the butter-basted turkey, cooked golden brown and filling the entire house with its mouth-watering aroma. That is the "good part" of the Thanksgiving meal.

Without intimate fellowship with Christ, the Christian life is just a buffet of so many side dishes and relish trays. We've all stood in that line at one time or another, only to come to the end of the line, disappointed. And who of us wants to go through that again?

Responding to the Moment

Personalize the Passage

Now that we've reflected on the passage, we move to the step of responding to it in a personal way.

In his excellent book, *Reaching Out*, Henri Nouwen discusses the importance of personalizing the Scriptures. "Reading the scriptures is not as easy as it seems since in our academic world we tend to make anything and everything we read subject to analysis and discussion. But the word of God should lead us first of all to contemplation and meditation. Instead of taking the words apart, we should bring them together in our innermost being; instead of wondering if we agree or disagree, we should wonder which words are directly spoken to us and connect directly with our most personal story. Instead of thinking about the words as potential subjects for an interesting dialogue or paper, we should be willing to let them penetrate into the most hidden corners of our heart, even to those places where no other word has yet found entrance. Then and only then can the word bear fruit as seed sown in rich soil. Only then can we really 'hear and understand.'"[2]

So how do we do that?

By asking questions, questions that now turn from the biblical text to the text of our daily lives.

How do we keep from missing the good part of the meal Jesus has prepared for us?

Christ's advice to Martha is advice to all of us who struggle in this area. "Martha, Martha, you are worried and bothered about so many things. Only a few things are necessary, really only one. And Mary has chosen the better part, which shall not be taken from her."

Christ is telling us, as well as Martha, that we need to simplify our lives, focusing on the one thing that matters so that our passion for Him can have an opportunity to grow.

He is telling us that we can get distracted from Him even in the midst of serving Him. Like Martha, we can take our eyes off of the One we're serving and onto all of our preparations, whether that's meal preparations or sermon preparations. Like Martha, we can get angry, even in our volunteer work, that someone has left us to do all the serving alone. Like Martha, we can stomp out of the kitchen, into some committee meeting, and start telling people off.

The vacation Anne Morrow Lindbergh once took on an East Coast beach, which she chronicled in her book, *Gift from the Sea*, offers an excellent model for reflective living. It is full of wit and wisdom and rich reflections about life. In this reflection she raises the same question the Mary and Martha passage raises, showing how universal the struggle is.

"I begin to understand," she writes, "why the saints were rarely married women. I am convinced it has nothing inherently to do, as I once supposed, with chastity or children. It has to do primarily with distractions. The bearing, rearing, feeding and educating of children; the running of a house with its thousand details; human relationships with their myriad pulls—woman's normal occupations in general run counter to creative life, or contemplative life, or saintly life. The problem is not merely one of *Woman and Career, Woman and the Home, Woman and Independence*. It is more basically: how to remain whole in the midst of the distractions of life. . . ."[3]

How *do* we remain whole in the midst of the distractions of life? It's a question we all wrestle with. But for Christians the question goes deeper.

In the midst of the distractions of life, how do we remain wholly devoted to Christ?

We do what Mary did.

We make a choice to sit at Christ's feet. That is where the "many things" we are involved in are brought into submission to the "one thing that is necessary."

In his book, *A Testament of Devotion*, Thomas Kelly tells how we do that. "Many of the things we are doing seem so important to us. We haven't been able to say No to them, because they seemed so important. But if we *center down*, as the old phrase goes, and live in that holy Silence which is deeper than life, and take our life program into the silent places of the heart, with complete openness, ready to do, ready to renounce according to His leading, then many of the things we are doing lose their vitality for us."[4]

To Christ's feet we bring the "many things" in our life for His scrutiny. There we submit to Him our plans, our goals, our dreams, our work, our opportunities, our schedules, and we ask Him, "Which ones, Lord? Which things would you want me to do? In which activities can I serve you best? What work would be the best stewardship of the gifts with which you have entrusted me? What should I say yes to, Lord? And to what should I say no?"

Then we wait for His answer. Which often doesn't come right away but in His own time and in His own way. The farther we are from His feet, the harder it will be to hear that answer. In a busy kitchen, it is almost impossible.

That choice to get busy or to sit still, to work in the kitchen or to wait at Christ's feet, is essentially a decision whether or not to submit the details of our life to His lordship. If we decide to submit them, it simplifies our life because it puts us accountable to one master instead of to a pantheon of competing ones.

Pray Through the Passage

After we've gone through the process of responding to the Scriptures personally, we respond to them now prayerfully. In keeping with the overarching goal of seeking to enflesh the Great Commandment in our day-to-day lives, we reach both upward and outward. We reach upward in prayer and outward in practice.

The following prayer grew out of my reflections on this passage.

Dear Savior at whose feet I now sit,

When you knock on the door to my heart, what is it you are looking for? What is it you want? Is it not to come in to dine with me and I with you? Is it not for fellowship?

And yet, so often, where do you find me? At your feet? No. In the kitchen. How many times have I become distracted and left you there . . . sitting . . . waiting . . . longing?

What is so important about my kitchen full of preparations that draws me away from you? How can they seem so trivial now and yet so urgent when I'm caught up in them?

Forgive me for being so distracted by my preparations and so little attracted by your presence. For being so diligent in my service and so negligent in my devotions. For being so quick to my feet and so slow to yours.

Help me to understand that it is an intimate moment you seek from me, not an elaborate meal.

Guard my heart this day from the many distractions that vie for my attention. And help me to fix my eyes on you. Not on my rank in the kingdom, as did the disciples. Not on the finer points of theology, as did the scribes. Not on the sins of others, as did the Pharisees. Not on a place of worship, as did the woman at the well. Not on the budget, as did Judas. But on you.

Bring me out of the kitchen, Lord. Bid me come to your feet. And there may I thrill to sit and adore thee. . . .[5]

Give the Passage a Place to Live in Our Heart

In his book, *Life Together,* Dietrich Bonhoeffer sheds some important light on the process of reflecting on the Word. "It is not necessary that we should discover new ideas in our meditation. Often this only diverts us and feeds our vanity. It is sufficient if the Word, as we read and understand it, penetrates and dwells within us. As Mary 'pondered in her heart' the things that were told by the shepherds, as what we have casually overheard follows us for a long time, sticks in our mind, occupies, disturbs, or delights us, without our ability to do anything about it, so in meditation God's Word seeks to enter in and remain with us. It strives to stir us, to work and operate in us, so that we shall not get away from it the whole day long. Then it will do its work in us, often without our being conscious of it."[6]

Here is where the internalized seed begins its outward growth, changing our priorities and submitting them to Christ. Generally this doesn't happen overnight. It's a process of growth. When we give the Word of God space to live in our heart, the Spirit of God will cause it to take root, penetrating the earthiest recesses of our lives. Who can be sure how deeply its roots will burrow within us or how broadly its branches will extend beyond us? But if we give the Word space in the garden, of this we can be sure. The Holy Spirit will entwine the passage around the trellis of our life and apply it in ways we never could have imagined, vining its way not only to the lives of those around us but even to those down from us, across generations.

Such is the potential of the seed.

And the power of the Spirit that stimulates its growth.

Reflecting on Movies

Christ's admonition that we stop worrying about the splinters in our brother's eye and, instead, remove the log from our own, gives timeless weight and testimony to the phenomenon of projection. . . . We magnify the capabilities of our friends and strangers, positive and negative, then feel ineffectual and wanting in their midst. Thus we escape the consequences of our potential and miss the mark of responsible, truthful engagement with our own experience.

Film (indeed all the arts) lets us see ourselves anew. Movies can show us where we store our "logs." [1]

MARSHA SINETAR

Reel Power: Spiritual Growth Through Film

I n his book, *Experiment in Criticism*, C.S. Lewis says: "A work of (whatever) art can be either 'received' or 'used.' When we 'receive' it we exert our senses and imagination and various other powers according to a pattern invented by the artist. When we 'use' it we treat it as assistance for our own activities."[2]

The difference between using and receiving what the arts have to offer is the difference between art criticism and art appreciation. When we judge art, we stand above it, as a critic. When we appreciate art, we sit below it, as a student. The one is the posture of the proud. The other, the place of the humble.

Humility is what puts us in a place to receive all the good that God has to offer in this life. Some of that goodness comes through the arts.

Think back when you were a child and to some of the moments where you were deeply moved. Were not some of those moments through some form of art? A photograph. A song like "Somewhere Over the Rainbow." A Robert Frost poem. A movie like *Bambi*. A book like *The Yearling*.

Who knows what moment God may use in our lives today or how He may use it. But unless we are open to the moment and receptive to it, we will never know. And maybe that, in part, is why Jesus told the disciples to humble themselves as a little child.

Because there is one thing a child is particularly good at that an adult is not.

The ability to receive a gift.

I have, over the years since my childhood, received a number of gifts from the hands of the various arts. Of those hands, none has been as generous to me with its gifts as the movies. Movies are particularly good at helping us live more reflective lives. Movies give us a couple of hours in the dark, to laugh, to cry, to think, to lose ourselves in someone else's story. What they do, better than any medium, is help us to see. The way the camera moves in for a close-up, emphasizing something important. The way the film speed slows down, extending a moment so we can experience it more fully. And with the advent of video, we can watch a scene over and over, savoring every second, something we can't often do in real life.

If we learn to see there, in a movie, it is likely we will learn to see elsewhere. That's why I love the movies. They help us to see life. Sometimes if we look at people a little more closely than we normally do, or from a little farther away, or from a different angle, or from another time, say, when they were kids, we see something in them that maybe we have never seen before.

And maybe that something we have never seen before is precisely the something that helps us love them as perhaps we were never able to before.

It doesn't always happen in a movie, but when it does, it's a wonderful experience.

I had that experience when I saw the movie *Fried Green Tomatoes*. I've seen it many times, and each time it seems I see something I didn't see the time before. One scene in particular stands out.

Reading the Moment

I wish I could show you the scene, because showing is always more powerful than telling. I encourage you to rent the movie and watch it for yourself, paying particular attention to this scene at the Whistle Stop Cafe. The time is lunch. The restaurant is packed, which is good because Idgy and her friend Ruth bought the restaurant with borrowed money. They are very much Mary and Martha types of characters. Idgy is the bustling, outspoken one. Ruth, the more relaxed, quiet one.

Idgy is waiting on tables, dropping off a plate of cornbread at one table, filling up coffee cups at another. All the while, Grady, the town sheriff, is following in her wake, trying to talk some sense into her. He's trying to get her to realize that her giving away food to black people in the backyard of the restaurant is causing talk among the paying, white customers. Of course, what makes sense to Grady is nonsense to Idgy. Ruth, meanwhile, is behind the counter, watching all this, listening, not knowing how her outspoken partner is going to handle the sheriff's complaints.

"Some pie, Grady?" Ruth interrupts, trying to diffuse the situation.

But even pie can't sidetrack Grady. The conversation goes back and forth between Grady and Idgy, but Idgy isn't stopping to give him the time of day, let alone an explanation for her actions. It's lunch hour at the Whistle Stop Cafe, the busiest time of day, and she has more pressing things to deal with.

At least for the moment.

Then the moment changes. As she goes back to the kitchen to fix more coffee, her eye catches a hand trembling at the lunch counter. The hand belongs to Smokey Lonesome, a homeless transient that has been hanging around town. Idgy had fixed him a plate full of fried chicken, mashed potatoes, and corn, and as he is bringing a fork full of corn to his mouth, his hand is shaking so badly that the corn is falling off.

The camera cuts to Ruth, watching.

Idgy stops what she's doing and comes over to him. "Come on outside, Smokey," she says quietly. And as she walks him out the back door, Smokey apologizes for what happened and tells her, "I'll be movin' on now."

At that moment Idgy pulls out a pint of whiskey from her apron and gives it to him to help calm his DTs, puts an arm around him as they walk, and tells him a story. The story is one her brother used to joke with her about when she was a young girl, a story about a pond freezing while a flock of ducks was on it, and how the ducks flew off to Georgia and took the pond with them.

The camera catches Ruth watching all this through the screen door.

The next moment we see is late at night with Smokey lying down in their storage shed. Into the shed comes Ruth, with a blanket she drapes over him.

"God bless you, ma'am," Smokey says, and the scene ends.

That is the *reading* of the scene, so to speak. Here are some of my thoughts as I reflected on it.

Reflecting on the Moment

I thought about the scene because I was touched by it. Something in my heart resonated with what I saw, telling me to pay attention, that something sacred was at stake here. I think what touched me was that I saw something of Jesus in the scene.

It took me off guard, because I wasn't expecting Him to show up in a movie. Jesus comes to us, I've learned, sometimes in the most unlikely of ways, which, if we're not looking, we'll miss. He comes to us in ways that require more than our eyes to see. He speaks to us in ways that require more than our ears to hear. He comes to us in ways that require the whole of us to respond, because it is to the whole of us that He makes His appeal.

In this case, Jesus comes in the form of Idgy Threadgood.

Idgy is a nonconformist. She ridicules organized religion, openly defies authority, smokes cigars, drinks, gambles, curses like a sailor sometimes. But underneath all that, something of Jesus emerged. My guess is that you saw it, too, even before I brought it to your attention. When Idgy took Smokey Lonesome outside, put her arm around him, and told him a story, it seemed the sort of thing Jesus would have done. Maybe Jesus would have given him a different drink or told him a different story, but the gestures of kindness were the same, weren't they?

Did you see Jesus anywhere else?

In Ruth.

When she covered Smokey Lonesome with the blanket. Although the scene focused on Idgy, first with Idgy and Grady, then with Idgy and Smokey, at different moments in the scene the camera cut to Ruth as she watched Idgy. And the compassion she saw in Idgy brought out the compassion in her.

Did you see Jesus anywhere else in this scene?

He's a little harder to see in this character, so you'll have to squint. Stop here and read through the scene once more to see if you can spot Him.

❧

Give up?

Maybe this will help. I've found in looking at art that sometimes what the artist was trying to capture is hard to see. In cases like that it helps to read the artist's caption under the painting. The caption that the Spirit brought to mind in this case is found in Matthew 25:37-40.

> Then the righteous will answer Him, saying, "Lord, when did we see You hungry, and feed You, or thirsty, and give You drink? And when did we see You a stranger, and invite You in, or naked, and clothe You? And when did we see You sick, or in prison, and come to You?"
>
> And the King will answer and say to them, "Truly I say to you, to the extent that you did it to one of these brothers of Mine, even the least of them, you did it to Me."

The picture is perfectly clear after the caption, isn't it?

Of course, it's Smokey Lonesome.

Now a question for *your* reflection. How do these three characters relate to each other in the spiritual realm?

I'll give you a minute . . .

❧

In them is formed the dynamic whereby Christ is formed in us.

Idgy is the mature Christ living among us.

Ruth is the emerging Christ.

Smokey Lonesome is the needy Christ.

It was the needy Christ in Smokey who called to the mature Christ in Idgy who called to the emerging Christ in Ruth. Each helped the other. The needy Christ helped the mature Christ to be made visible among them. The mature Christ, made visible, helped the emerging Christ by way of example. When the emerging Christ followed that example, the needy Christ was visited. Through Idgy and Ruth, Smokey was not turned away with a "Go-in-peace" prayer. He went away warmed and filled. And through Smokey, they did, too.

"God bless you, ma'am."

The blessing went both ways. To him back to her. A circle of sorts. And that is how the emerging Body of Christ grows and how the mature Body is made visible to the world.

Question: Can you think of any modern-day example that parallels the dynamic between Idgy, Ruth, and Smokey Lonesome?

This may take more than a minute . . .

Stumped? Here's a hint. "The poorest of the poor"

Mother Teresa. She's Idgy. And the poorest of the poor, whom she served in India, they are the Smokey Lonesomes.

Now here's the hard part.

Who is Ruth's counterpart?

Hint: She died the same week Mother Teresa did.

Princess Di.

During one sad week in September of 1997, we were barraged with pictures of Princess Diana and Mother Teresa. Both funerals were covered by the media. Newspapers, tabloids, and magazines rushed to hit the newsstands, each with their own exclusive editions. One of those editions was particularly poignant. It was *Life* magazine's special tribute to Diana. The magazine juxtaposed photos of the two women with this comment: "Life seldom linked Mother Teresa, 87, and Princess Diana, 36, despite a much-reproduced photograph of their last meeting, earlier this year. But an accident of timing links them in death. Rarely had the founder of the Missionaries of Charity seemed so much a celebrity, or the Princess of Wales so saintly. Comparisons that would otherwise never have occurred suddenly felt inevitable."[3]

Years earlier, Mother Teresa had invited Princess Di to come to Calcutta, but before she came there, she came to Rome, where the nun had been hospitalized. The two met several times after that. Finally Diana did come to Calcutta, where she dispensed medicine to the sick, along with candy and little gestures of kindness. From the moment of their first meeting, Princess Diana considered Mother Teresa her mentor.

In *U.S. News & World Report,* Michael Satchell noted the similarities between the two: "In an age of celebrity worship, there were common points in the lives of the tiny, wizened woman and the willowy, beautiful princess, even as their deaths drew a poignant and ironic counterpoint. Adored by millions, the tragic, privileged Diana was sanctified as much for her beauty and fame as for her willingness to reject the stiff traditions of British Royalty and openly embrace the sick and handicapped. Mother Teresa, whose Missionaries of Charity minister to millions of people worldwide, was revered as a 'living saint' whose lifetime of caring for the destitute and the dying earned her the Nobel Peace Prize in 1979.

"The two women shared a compassion for the less fortunate and a deep love for children. Their final meeting took place last June at the Missionaries of Charity convent in the Bronx. The ailing missionary stepped out of her wheel chair to stroll with Diana. Arm in arm, the pair kissed, hugged, and prayed in a scene the British press dubbed as the most remarkable royal walkabout ever."[4]

Mother Teresa and Princess Diana.

Idgy and Ruth.

Beautiful, isn't it? The dynamic of love. And how Christ is made visible to the world (Ephesians 4:11-16).

Now another question.

Responding to the Moment

Which role would you want to play in the movie?

I'll give you another minute . . .

❧

. . . and I bet you had fifty-nine seconds left over.

Idgy. In a heartbeat. She's strong and cute and has a good personality. A real leader. Ruth would be an okay part. She's cute, too, and the potential in other areas of her life is emerging. Either one, but preferably Idgy.

Say you're not offered either one. Say the only role you're offered is Smokey Lonesome's. Would you take it?

In the movie, sure. It's a bit part, but it could lead to other things, bigger parts, better roles.

How about in real life?

Any takers?

You're not seeing my hand go up either. And yet God may call me at some time in my life, as He may call you at some time in yours, to play the role of the needy Christ. Would you if He did? Would I?

Honestly?

Honestly, I want to be like Christ.

But honestly, I want to be like the Christ who turned the water into wine, not the Christ who thirsted on a cross. I want to be the clothed Christ, not the one whose garment was stripped and gambled away. I want to be the Christ who fed the five thousand, not the one who hungered for forty days in the wilderness. I want to be the free Christ, walking through wheatfields with His disciples, not the imprisoned Christ who was deserted by them.

I want to be the Good Samaritan, not the man who fell among thieves.

But if the man had not fallen among thieves, been beaten, stripped, and left for dead, the good in the Samaritan never would have emerged.

This is the dark side of Christianity, the side we don't see when we sign up. That if we want to be like Christ, we have to embrace both sides of His life. What else could it mean when the Bible talks about "the fellowship of His suffering?" How could we enter that fellowship *apart* from suffering? How could we truly know the man of sorrows acquainted with grief if we had not ourselves known grief and sorrow?

That is how Christ grows in us, both corporately as a body and individually as members of that body. It is also the way many people come to Christ. For some people, it is the only way. And perhaps that explains, at least partially, why bad things sometimes happen to good people.

For the sake of those around them.

That they might come to Christ.

That Christ might come to them, to live in them.

So that once again a Savior can be born into the world.

Reflecting on Other People

[God] also speaks to us about ourselves, about what he wants us to do and what he wants us to become; and this is the area where I believe that we know so much more about him than we admit even to ourselves, where people hear God speak even if they do not believe in him. A face comes toward us down the street: Do we raise our eyes or do we keep them lowered, passing by in silence? Somebody says something about somebody else, and what he says happens to be not only cruel but also funny, and everybody laughs. Do we laugh too, or do we speak the truth? When a friend has hurt us, do we take pleasure in hating him, because hate has its pleasures as well as love, or do we try to build back some flimsy little bridge? Sometimes when we are alone, thoughts come swarming into our heads like bees—some of them destructive, ugly, self-defeating thoughts, some of them creative and glad. Which thoughts do we choose to think then, as much as we have the choice? Will we be brave today or a coward today? Not in some big way probably but in some little foolish way, yet brave still? Will we be honest today or a liar? Just some pint-sized honesty, but honest still. Will we be a friend or cold as ice today?

All the absurd little meetings, decisions, inner skirmishes that go to make up our days. It all adds up to very little, and yet it all adds up to very much. Our days are full of nonsense, and yet not, because it is precisely into the nonsense of our days that God speaks to us words of great significance. . . ."[1]

FREDERICK BUECHNER

The Magnificent Defeat

To better love God and other people is the goal of the reflective life. But before we can love them, we must see them. And we must see them not as we would like to see them or as they would like to be seen. We must see them as they are. Otherwise we don't love the person. We love the image we perceive the person to be. If we are to love people as they are, we must see them as they are. Which means seeing all that lies hidden within them.

There is a story of a rabbi sitting in his study, when his reading is interrupted by a knock on the door.

"Come in."

It was one of his students who was so grateful for his teacher he simply had to come and tell him.

"I just wanted you to know, Rabbi, how much I love you."

The rabbi put down his book and looked over his glasses.

"What hurts me?"

The student looked at him quizzically. "What?"

"What hurts me?" the rabbi asked again.

The boy stood there, speechless, finally shrugging his shoulders. "I don't know."

"How can you love me," the rabbi asked, "if you don't know what hurts me?"

What hurts you, and do the people who love you know it? If not, how can they truly love you? Or me? How can we love one another if we don't know what hurts us?

Like what hurt Stevie. Stevie is a teenage girl who is the life of the party, always up, always in a good mood, always making other people laugh. Here is her hurt.

Do you know what it's like
to be a clown?
Do you know what it's like
to suffer
from too many laughs?
Do you know what it's like
for a girl
to be born a circus act?
Do you know what it's like
to have a funny bone
for a brain?
Do you?

I don't have any white paint
on my face
but I wear a mask.
I have a silly smile
that never changes.
It's always there
and everyone expects it
to be there.
They like it that way.
They enjoy a clown
and they use a clown

because they think

a clown doesn't care

about anything.

I can't enjoy a bad mood

with other people.

That's a strange luxury.

I have to be a clown.

Whenever people tease me

I turn into an act,

a fool standing on my head.

Then I look up

and I see a world full

of upside-down people

trying to be

what they aren't.

I see so many people

wearing strange colorless makeup,

and the longer they wear it

the harder it is to discover

what kind of people they really are,

underneath.

I'm waiting for someone

to step behind my face

and find me!

Not Stevie, but me!

Lord,

when will this Stevie

be free

to be me? [2]

When *will* we be free?

When somebody steps behind our face and finds us. And loves us, despite what they see there. Most of the time, though, most of us don't even bother to look. And if we do, chances are it won't take long before we look away. And stay away. Because sometimes what we see inside another person repulses us rather than attracts us. That's why we wear masks.

Sometimes, though, when the mask comes down, so do our prejudices and the distance we have kept because of them.

I'm thinking of Madonna.

Everyone knows Madonna. The singer. The pop icon. The bad girl of MTV. Everyone knows her. Sean Penn's ex-wife. Dennis Rodman's born-to-be-wild girlfriend. David Letterman's foulmouthed guest.

Everyone knows. She's the movie star. The author of that sex book. The one who talked her trainer into inseminating her.

Everyone knows Madonna.

Or do we?

I thought I did. Until an interview I saw on television.

Reading the Moment

The interviewer was asking Madonna the regular stock questions, to which she gave the regular stock answers. And the two of them were sitting there, going back and forth like that until the interviewer prefaced her next question something like this: "You're a woman who has it all. You're a singer, actress, author. You've got money, fame, a place in American pop culture. You've been on the cover of almost every magazine. You're not just a global figure, you're a global force."

Meanwhile, Madonna is sitting there, taking all this in, kind of nodding. Until the question.

"Is there anything you would give it all up for?"

Suddenly Madonna's face froze. Her eyes brimmed with tears. Her lip quivered. She took a breath, then answered.

"To have a mom."

Reflecting on the Moment

I didn't know she had lost her mom when she was little. And I didn't know how much that had hurt her. But the tears told me something of how badly it hurt. So did her answer.

As I watched her sitting there slumped in her chair, almost like a little girl, I felt a sudden tenderness for her. Then I understood. Madonna got pregnant so she could be a mommy to a little girl, the mommy she never had. Seeing the hurt inside Madonna helped me to love her. And to pray for her. And to wait with a hopeful sense of expectancy to see how that baby would change her over the years.

I didn't have to wait long. While standing in line at the grocery store, I saw her picture on the cover of *TV Guide*, the words printed over her picture: "Madonna Confidential." I wondered if what she had to say in *TV*

Guide helped to explain the tears I saw in her television interview. Here's an excerpt. See for yourself.

TVG: Friends say you are a more peaceful person since the baby.

Madonna: When I went to the hospital I remember thinking: "I don't have a baby right now. But in a couple of hours, I'm going to have a baby. So I will be a totally different person." I just think it is like crossing the border.

TVG: Into feminine territory.

Madonna: Yeah! I think it made me face up to my more feminine side. I had a much more masculine view of the world. Divide and conquer. I grew up without a mother, and I have always had this real kind of I-don't-need-anybody-and-I-will-never-rely-on-anybody attitude about the world. You always have your guard up. And you can't really do that with a child.

TVG: Did having a child, particularly a girl, help you heal the hurt you felt about losing your mother at such a young age?

Madonna: It had an incredible effect. What I missed and longed for was that unconditional love that a mother gives you. And so having my daughter is that same kind of thing. It's like that first true, pure unconditional love. It is the first time it has happened to me that I am aware of. . . .[3]

Responding to the Moment

If you judged Madonna on appearances, as I had done, you wouldn't have seen the hurt inside. And if you can't see the hurt, how can you love her?

I believe when Jesus walked this earth, He saw the hurts inside. The woman at the well. The woman with seven demons. The woman caught in adultery. By all appearances they were trashy women. But Jesus looked beyond appearances. He saw the hurt inside. And He touched it, ever-so-gently, to bring healing and wholeness.

If we are to be like Him, we too must look beyond appearances, beyond the sleazy clothes and the trashy talk and the tabloid gossip about other people's lives. We have to see inside, to the hurt inside. And somehow we have to reach inside, ever-so-gently touching the hurt to bring whatever healing we can.

It was the hurt of losing her mother that sent Madonna searching for love. It is, I believe, the love of God she was searching for, what we all are searching for.

From the interview I learned that Madonna's search has taken her to a branch of Judaism, which she is presently studying and practicing. And who knows, if she keeps up the search, where it will lead?

Maybe to Jesus.

And maybe all along it was He who had been searching for her.

Reflecting on the Theater

[Drama] gives the essence of life, and in three hours it speaks volumes. It warns and counsels, teaches justice and keeps alive pity. It celebrates man's liberty and his struggles, and all that is noble wanders into it. It enlists the sympathies to such an extent that the listener is his own poet. It analyzes all motives, withholding nothing, lays bare everything. It is in fact the plainest, most direct of all forms of teaching. It does not formulate morals in words, but in deeds; and if life, which is the drama, is not a constant mentor, unheeded also in its teachings, what is it?[1]

W. T. PRICE

The Technique of Drama

quoted in *Self Culture for Young People,* edited by Andrew Sloan Draper

Parables were what Jesus used when Israel rejected His clear and forthright teaching (Matthew 13:10-16). They served the dual function of revealing truth to hearts that were receptive and concealing it from those that were not. Maybe that is one of the reasons why God doesn't seem to speak so clearly at this time in the history of the church. Maybe He is speaking, but it is more in parables.

He speaks to us through parables in nature, I believe. Their truth, though hidden, is everywhere, if only we have the eyes to see. Like sunshine and rain, the sacred permeates the earth. Like seeds on the ground, parables are everywhere, holding the secrets of heaven clutched in their tiny hands.

God speaks to us through other parables besides in nature. He speaks the language of parable in history, in dreams, often in the everyday moments of our lives. Every once in a while even in a movie.

The movie *Camelot* is full of parables, many of them so biblical they seem to come right out of the Book of Proverbs. One of my favorite scenes is at the end of the movie where King Arthur is preparing for battle. Lancelot's troops, which had defected from the Round Table and divided the kingdom, are preparing to fight Arthur's troops. As the king puts on his armor, a rustling in the bushes catches his attention. He draws his sword, but as it turns out, it is only a boy in hiding. The boy's name is Tom, from the faraway village of Warwick. He comes with a childlike sort of courage, wanting to fight as a knight of the Round Table. Arthur asks him if he ever knew a knight. The boy answers no. Ever saw a knight? No. How then did he hear of the Round Table?

"From the stories that were told," the boy replies.

That is when Arthur knights him Sir Tom of Warwick, sending him not into battle but to run behind the lines. To run and to live. And to return home where he can tell the stories of that "one brief shining moment" that was Camelot.

The writer is a custodian of the stories once spoken around campfires, around Passover tables, communion tables. Stories we are admonished not to forget. A storyteller has the task of running behind the lines to make sure the stories live, to make sure that those shining moments of our humanity, however brief, are not forgotten.

To keep them fashionable for each generation, though, some stories over the years have been given new clothes. And so *Romeo and Juliet* becomes *West Side Story*. And the story of the Prodigal Son becomes *Where the Wild Things Are* by Maurice Sendak. The most compelling story in the Bible was given new clothes by French writer Victor Hugo. Which in turn was given a newer set of clothes by Andrew Lloyd Webber.

One night at the Shubert Theatre in Los Angeles, I saw the Andrew Lloyd Webber play, *Les Misérables*, which was adapted from the Hugo novel, published in 1862. "This is a religious book," Hugo wrote in an unpublished preface to the book. The Andrew Lloyd Webber play captures the spirit of its religious themes.

The play touched me profoundly. It was a deeply spiritual experience. Who would have thought it? There in the entertainment capital of the world. The next day I wrote about the experience in my journal. Here are some of my reflections, which centered more about life in general:

> The sets, the songs, the story—everything was outstanding. I was moved to tears at several points during the play. And I felt a lure, a calling from beyond the barricades of this earth. Distant yet distinct. Calling in an ever-mounting crescendo of conviction . . . that life is too short to be trivial, too precious to be squandered.

Two days later I made another journal entry after listening to the music of *Les Mis* on a CD player at work. This time my reflections took me to a deeper place to consider my own life in particular:

> What a great legacy to leave behind, a story that stirs the soul and takes you by the hand to the borders of the seen world to glimpse for a fleeting moment the glory of the world unseen. It quickened my determi-

nation to write novels. And yet, I seem to be getting such a late start on it all that it is depressing. There are so many novels to read and to learn from before I feel I can do much. There is such little time left—30, 40 years at most. Half my life is now over. I'll be 38 in a month. My knees are getting worse every year and constantly ache. The arthritic spur on my neck. The ringing in my ear and the slow erosion of my hearing. And yesterday I finally got some new glasses—bifocals no less.

I had no idea my reflections on the play would lead me to thinking about my own mortality, but they did. And I think that was good, because it caused me to measure my days, reflecting not only on how many at best I had to spend but how I was spending them. The music on the CD allowed me to hear all the lyrics, some of which I had missed in the live performance. And playing it over and over again helped to give the story a greater place to live in my heart, where it deepened its roots.

Reading the Moment

The story of *Les Misérables*, if you're not familiar with it, is a contrast between law and grace. The protagonist is a man named Jean Valjean, who represents a life lived by grace. The antagonist is a police officer named Javert, who represents a life driven by the dictates of the law. Javert's life was a relentless quest, without rest, without peace, that eventually drove him to suicide. Valjean's life, in contrast, unfolded like a slow-blossoming flower, a soft-petaled act of love at a time. Quiet. Unpretentious. Yet its beauty was undeniable; its fragrance, irresistible.

One of his acts of love was to a sick and impoverished woman named Fantine. She tells the tragic story of her life in a heartrending song.

There was a time when men were kind,
When their voices were soft
And their words inviting.
There was a time when love was blind
And the world was a song
And the song was exciting.
There was a time.
Then it all went wrong.[2]

For people in the bud of youth, life seems forever spring. But autumn comes to all of our lives. And sometimes it wilts the most hopeful of dreams. As it did Fantine's.

I had a dream my life would be
So different from this hell I'm living,
So different now from what it seemed.
Now life has killed
The dream I dreamed.[3]

The song brought not only applause but tears. The applause came in response to the beauty of the song and how well it was sung. But the tears, the tears came from someplace else. Someplace deeper. For who of us has not felt at some time or another the way Fantine felt? If we have lived long enough and honestly enough, a chord trembles within us when we hear Fantine's song, when we see her fall into an anguished heap in the middle of the stage. For who of us has not had a dream of what we thought our lives would be, only to wake up and find it so different from the hell we have all at some time or another had to live?

Valjean vows to the dying Fantine that he will find her daughter Cosette and raise her as his own. Under his care, Cosette grows up and blossoms into a beautiful young woman. She meets a young man named Marius, they fall in love, and become engaged. But revolution breaks out in France, and Marius goes off to fight. Valjean's prayer for Marius again brought tears.

God on high,
Hear my prayer—
In my need
You have always been there. . . .

He is young,
He is only a boy,
You can take,
You can give—
Let him be,
Let him live. . . .
Bring him home.[4]

God does bring Marius home, and the two young lovers marry. But the years have taken their toll on Valjean, and he finds himself being brought home—his heavenly home. In the finale, he sings as he goes to his death.

Take my hand
And lead me to salvation.
Take my love

For love is everlasting.
And remember
The truth that once was spoken,
To love another person
Is to see the face of God.[5]

In the finale the entire cast came onstage to sing of a time when all of earth's battles will be over.

They will live again in freedom
In the garden of the Lord,
They will walk behind the plough-share,
They will put away the sword.
The chain will be broken
And all men will have their reward.[6]

Then, with almost evangelistic fervor, the singers appealed to the audience.

Will you join in our crusade?
Who will be strong and stand with me?
Somewhere beyond the barricade
Is there a world you long to see?[7]

The standing ovation of the audience seemed a collective prayer. *Please, God, if there is a world beyond the barricade of this one, please, show us a glimpse of it, take our hand and lead us there. Please, God, take our hand and lead us to salvation.*

Am I romanticizing the evening?

I don't think so. I think within all of us is an artesian hope that in a moment of grace surfaces through our tears. The hope that there is a world beyond this one. That it is a world where God reigns. And that He is a God of love who will one day take our hand and lead us there.

The sets, the songs, the story, everything was so stirring to my soul. That night at the theater I was given a glimpse of that world beyond the barricade. And that night, heaven seemed somehow not only more real but more wonderful.

That night I came to the theater, I left differently. In three hours something inside me changed, a conversion of sorts.

Often we emphasize that conversion takes place in a moment of conception when the divine initiative and the human response embrace. But that is just the start of the new creation. Day by day, each cell of that new life is renewed and enlarged. Moment by moment that gestating person is growing, changing, struggling to emerge into the fullness of life.

That is what George MacDonald meant, I think, when he said: "As the world must be redeemed in a few men to begin with, so the soul is redeemed in a few of its thoughts, and works, and ways to begin with: it takes a long time to finish the new creation of this redemption."[8]

Reflecting on the Moment

What a story Victor Hugo wrote. What a service Andrew Lloyd Webber performed in bringing it back to life. The play showed me how living by grace, as Jean Valjean did, is such a more beautiful way of living life than by law, as did the police officer, Javert.

But how did a life like Valjean's happen? What made him the man he was?

The story begins when Valjean is released from prison after years of incarceration. His crime? He had stolen a loaf of bread during the years of famine before the French Revolution. When released, he wandered from town to town. In every town he is shunned. Who wants a transient shuffling through their streets? Who wants an ex-con snooping around the neighborhood, rummaging through their trash cans?

Door after door is slammed in his face. Until in one town a door finally opens. The door of a church. A bishop there invites him to stay the night, to sit at his table, to eat and rest his weary soul. At dinner, Valjean surreptitiously eyes the exquisite silverware. He could sneak out with it when everyone goes to sleep. Sell it on the street. Use the money to give himself a fresh start. Later, in the middle of the night, he does just that. Once he is on the street, though, two constables catch sight of the suspicious-looking stranger. They stop him, search him, find the stolen goods. And they take him back to the bishop.

The bishop's response is what changed Valjean's life, making him the man he was.

The bishop tells the officers he had given Valjean the silverware. As a gift. He then turns to Valjean and tells him how glad he is that he returned because he had forgotten to take the most valuable of all the silver pieces—the candlesticks.

That one act of love changes him. The changes are small at first, but day by day they continue. And for the rest of his days his life is spent showing love to others less fortunate than himself.

As I thought about that one act of love to a thief and how it forever changed his life, I couldn't help thinking, *This is the gospel, only in different clothes.* What Hugo said in a book and Webber said in a play, Paul said in a letter: "At one time we too were foolish, disobedient, deceived and enslaved by all kinds of passions and pleasures. We lived in malice and envy, being hated and hating one another. But when the kindness and love of God our Savior appeared, he saved us, not because of righteous things we had done, but because of his mercy" (Titus 3:3-5, NIV).

As I was reflecting about the bishop's kindness to a thief, another thief came to mind. I spent several days thinking about him. Here are some of those thoughts in light of the play.

Another time. Another thief. This time, though, the law wins. The crimes were witnessed. The verdict, handed down. The sentence, read. The sentence is slated to be carried out on Friday. There will be no appeals, no delays. Justice will be swift and certain. Death by crucifixion.

At this point I try to recreate the scene in my mind, as if I were part of the crowd, watching it all unfold. Sights. Sounds. Smells. I try to take in everything. For me, writing is a way of reflecting. Usually whatever insights I get, I get *while* I am writing, not before. So I write the scene with a sense of hopeful expectation . . .

Friday comes, and three prisoners are paraded through the narrow streets of Jerusalem. The cobbled stone road they stumble down wends outside the city walls to a chalky hill. To outsiders entering those walls, the hill billboards the message: Break the law, and this is what you'll get for it.

It takes six soldiers to wrestle the first prisoner onto the coarse beam of justice. Kicking and cursing, he flails against the splinters. But a boot to the face and one to the ribs causes him to suck in his defiance.

The sound of hammer against metal, and spikes bite his hands. His feet. Burly-armed soldiers hoist ropes that hang from the crossbeam like riggings from a mast. With each heave the spikes rasp bone, and pain cuts the air with the jaggedness of a primitive tool. The beam thuds into its hole, and once more pain slashes the air.

The crowd jostles for a better look as soldiers push the next prisoner to the ground. Spikes and screams. A thud and more screams.

Two down, one to go. This one is a Jew, a prophet of sorts. To the Roman Empire, He is little more than a judicial inconvenience. To the religious establishment, though, He is more than that. For His indictments have been a branding iron held against the self-righteous conscience of the nation. Scribes and Pharisees came away from the encounters with an unmistakable "H" seared on their foreheads, and now, maybe for the first time, everyone saw them for what they were—hypocrites.

Something had to be done with this irrepressible firebrand. And so something was.

A metal gavel rings out the sentence against Him. Stretched out on the wood, Jesus has surrendered His wrists to the judgment of the iron jury. The defendant is silent. He bargains no plea. Issues no threat. Utters no curse. His cross is lifted up, steadied into place, all the while His ribs carrying groans like hands cradling eggs.

The soldiers back away, except for a few huddled around a seamless garment owned by the Jew. Like dogs baring their teeth over a bone, the soldiers argue over who will get it. A game of chance, they agree, would be better than dividing it up. Winner take all.

But what they take is a rag compared to the covering Jesus gives.

"Father . . . forgive them . . . for they know not what they do."

The soldiers stop and look up. But only for a moment. Only until another soldier breaks the silence. "Come on, roll the dice." And they go back to their game.

The atmosphere surrounding the hilltop executions is like some grotesque circus. A place where the worst in the human heart is unleashed. Like a pack of ravenous hounds, the crowd circles the three trees of suspended flesh. One by one they lunge, and the thieves kick back the sharp-toothed words with curses.

The Jew in the middle, though, is silent. Which raises the hair on their backs even more. A wrinkling of lips. A hissing of insults. "You who are going to destroy the temple and build it in three days, save yourself!"

Another sneers. "Come down from the cross, if you are the Son of God!"

Jesus bears the sarcasm as He bears the nails biting his flesh.

Silently.

A few religious leaders nip at His feet. "He saved others, but He can't save Himself!"

"He's the King of Israel! Let Him come down from the cross, and we will believe in Him."

"He trusts in God. Let God rescue Him now if He wants Him, for He said, 'I am the Son of God.'"

The two thieves, relieved that the mouths have found other prey, join in. "Aren't you the Christ? Save yourself and us!"

But over time the one thief's thoughts turn inward. Toward the end, something softened him. Who's to say why? Maybe it was the nails that wore him down. Or the fever. Or the futility of resisting the inevitable.

Or was it something else?

He was a thief and a rebel, but he was guilty of so much more. He knew that. And he knew he was getting what he deserved. So was the other thief. But Jesus. What had He stolen? Whom had He killed? What had He done to deserve this?

"Father, forgive them . . ."

Are these the words of a criminal? The words of a rebel? Of a blasphemer?

If not, whose are they?

The thief's eyes angle toward the inscription. "THIS IS JESUS, THE KING OF THE JEWS."

Him, a king? The one hanging there, so helplessly, so powerlessly? Yet there is something about this man, something in His eyes, in His words, in the way He is taking it all. All the abuse. All the mockery. All the pain. Could it be true? The inscription above His head. Could there be a world beyond this one? A kingdom of some sort.

If so, could this be its king?

He takes a chance that it is. And with an empty, outstretched hand he makes a dying plea.

"Remember me . . . when you come into your kingdom."

But remember him for what? He is a thief. A hostile, foulmouthed thief. What is Jesus going to remember him for? For his goodness? His compassion? His contribution to society?

"Remember me," he pleads, not because of who he is but because of who Jesus is. And if Jesus could offer forgiveness to His enemies, maybe He would have something to offer him.

Jesus lifts His head. His hair is pasted darkly to His scalp. His hands, white and limp and numb. His life, seeping from the punctures in His head, His hands, His feet, from the lacerations on His back. His eyes, swollen from the pummeling abuse of Roman fists. With one arm outstretched to the thief, almost as if reaching for him, He says, "Today you will be with me in Paradise."

Think of how each of those fluid words of forgiveness must have felt on the parched lips of the dying man's soul.

Today. Not someday but this very day.

You will be with me. *You,* the thief. *You,* the guilty one, the condemned one, the outcast.

You *will* be with me. You have my word on it. I, not Roman law, will have the last word. And I say that you will have a future beyond the barricades of these wooden crosses.

And that future will be with *me.* Me, the King. The King of Kings and Lord of Lords. Whose throne is on the right hand of God.

And you will be with me . . . not on a cross . . . not in a tomb . . . not in some shadowy netherland of departed souls. You will be with me *in Paradise.* In the garden of God. Where there is no sin, no death. Where there are no tears. Where there is no reason to steal, for gold is so common it's used to pave streets, jewels so plentiful they're used as building materials. The river of life. The tree of life. The riches of heaven. They're yours. All yours.

In the farthest, wildest regions of our imagination can we even begin to comprehend what has happened? Can we see the incredible gift that has changed hands? Can we see both the greatness of the gift and the lowliness in which it was given?

　　Witness the majesty.

　　Witness the humility.

　　Witness the love of God

　　　　reaching down

　　　　　　and handing a common thief

　　　　　　　　the candlesticks.

Responding to the Moment

After reflecting on the play in light of this passage of Scripture, I realized that there is something of Jean Valjean and the thief on the cross in all of us. And it's the word *thief* that the Holy Spirit used to focus my thoughts and personalize my reflections, which follow.

We are thieves, too, you and I. We have stolen much in the short time we've passed through this neighborhood. Maybe it started by stuffing a little something into our pockets when no one was looking. A candy bar, say. Or a small toy. But later it was answers from someone else's homework. And still later, the pleasures from someone else's body. The sweet taste of stolen water or bread eaten in secret.

The pleasures, the passions. Lumped together, it's all just so much thievery, isn't it?

But there are other thefts we have been involved in. If we come clean, really clean, there's a lot more on our record, isn't there?

When we've raised our voices in anger, we've taken something away from peace. When we've lied, we've taken something from truth. When we've spoken the truth but not in love, we've taken something from God's kingdom by pushing someone a little farther away from its borders.

When we've been silent and withheld praise that was rightly due another person, we've stolen just as certainly as if we withheld wages from someone who has worked for them, sweated for them, sacrificed for them.

When we've been divisive, we've taken something away from the unity of a home or a church, an office or an organization. When we've been coercive, we've taken something away from another person's freedom. When we've been sarcastic, we've taken something away from another person's dignity.

With one hand we may have rendered unto Caesar the coin of taxation, but with the other we withheld the coins of respect, submission, and gratitude. When we demean the President, we take something not just from him but from the dignity of the office, and it leaves us all somehow a little poorer, a little less than we were before the joke, a little smaller than we were before the remark.

Somehow the image of God suffers a loss, too. Like the crazed man who took a hammer to the *Pieta* and shattered some of its marbled grandeur. He stole something, that man with the hammer. Not just something from the statue. And not just something from the Vatican. He stole something from Michelangelo, the creator, and, in the process, stole something from all of us.

The cutting remark made behind someone's back is not much different than the knife in the back of a mugging victim. Maybe that is why Jesus tells us in the Sermon on the Mount that murder and anger are members of the same gang, that if we call someone a fool, we have taken a stab at the very image of God and are perilously close to the most severe judgment.

Whether we've failed to give honor to the President or understanding to our mate or love to our neighbor, it's stealing. Isn't it? Isn't it really?

Anger, lies, lust, gossip. We've all had a hand in them. You. Me. All of us. For who of us has not done these things or thought these things at some time or another? A thief is a thief, whether he robs a liquor store with a gun or a corporation with a computer or someone's reputation with a rumor.

But they're such small, shoplifted things, aren't they? Such petty thefts. Besides, everybody does it.

But what may seem petty theft to us may be grand theft to God. And if the tongue was used in the robbery, then it's theft with a deadly weapon. We're all guilty. We just haven't been caught at it. We're all guilty. No one's put a finger on us in the line-up, that's all. We're all guilty. We just haven't been convicted.

But though our guilt is indefensible, God's grace is greater than our guilt. His kindness, greater than our disobedience. His emancipation, greater than our enslavement. His mercy, greater than our malice and envy. His love, greater than our hate. All of those are distilled in the words:

"Today you will be with me in Paradise."

Look closely.

It's a promise without conditions. Without exceptions. Without addenda. "Today you will be with me. . . ." Not if you're faithful. Not if you're obedient. Not if you measure up, pass inspection, make the grade.

You see, it's not an offer. It's a pronouncement. An edict. And a royal one at that. Signed in the King's own blood. Sealed with His own death. To all of us who've ever been caught red-handed with the silverware, those words are the candlesticks.

Candlesticks of the King.

And they're ours.

Forever.

What should our response be to such a gift?

To receive it, certainly. But how?

With the humility of one hanging on a cross.

Knowing that we are hanging there of our own doing.

Knowing that the gift offered us is not just our hope, it is our *only* hope.

And receiving it with such gratitude it forever changes how we live our lives, by extending to others the same kind of love that was extended to us.

PART VII

The Fruit of the Reflective Life

The fruit of the Spirit is love, joy, peace, patience, kindness, goodness, gentleness, self-control.

GALATIANS 5:22-23

I f the seeds sown in our heart are truly seeds from heaven, germinated by the Holy Spirit, we should expect at some time to see fruit. And that fruit should look very much like love, smell very much like joy, feel very much like peace, taste very much like patience.

The fruit of living a reflective life should be a changed life. The changes should affect not only who we are but how we live, branching from our soul to our schedule.

And it doesn't have to be a busy schedule to be a fruitful one.

"In our love for people are we to be excitedly hurried, sweeping all men and tasks into our loving concern?" asks Thomas Kelly in his book, *A Testament of Devotion.* "No," he says, "that is God's function. But He, working within us, portions out His vast concern into bundles, and lays on each of us our portion.

"And I find He never guides us into an intolerable scramble of panting feverishness. The Cosmic Patience becomes, in part, our patience, for after all God is at work in the world. It is not we alone who are at work in the world, frantically finishing a work to be offered to God.

"Life from the Center is a life of unhurried peace, and power. It is simple. It is serene. . . . We need not get frantic. He is at the helm. And when our little day is done we lie down quietly in peace, for all is well."[1]

Our Father's Heart

What Thomas Kelly puts into words, Psalm 131 puts into a picture.

O Lord, my heart is not proud, nor my eyes haughty;
Nor do I involve myself in great matters,
Or in things too difficult for me.
Surely I have composed and quieted my soul;
Like a weaned child rests against its mother,
My soul is like a weaned child within me. (vv. 1-2)

The picture evokes for me a fond memory.

When I was a little boy, my father would come home from work, sit on the couch, cross his legs, and read the newspaper. I mean, *really* read it. Cover to cover. Front page. Sports page. Business page. Even the classifieds. While he stretched out the paper in front of him, I would crawl in and out of the opening where his legs crossed. If he closed the opening by crossing his legs tighter, I would sit on his foot and use his leg as something of a rocking horse. By then, if he wasn't finished, I would crawl up next to him on the couch, leaning my head on his chest as he read. Sometimes I would stare at the newsprint or study the pictures. Other times I would simply close my eyes and rest. I remember many times just sitting there, my ear against his massive chest, listening to the beat of his heart. And resting there, I would try to breathe in sync with him, so that when he inhaled, I inhaled, and when he exhaled, I exhaled. No small feat for a little boy with a little chest. Still, I tried to keep up. And somehow—it's hard to explain why—it felt really good when I could.

Admiral Byrd recorded a similar feeling in his diary when he was exploring Antarctica during the winter of 1934. April 14. "I paused to listen to the silence. . . . The day was dying, the night being born—but with great peace. Here were imponderable processes and forces of the cosmos, harmonious and soundless. Harmony, that was it! That was what came out of the silence—a gentle rhythm, the strain of a perfect chord, the music of the spheres perhaps. It was enough to catch that rhythm, momentarily to be myself a part of it. In that instant I could feel no doubt of man's oneness with the universe."[2]

That's how I felt with my head against my father's chest, breathing in rhythm to his breathing. A sense of oneness with my father.

I felt that same sense of oneness every time we walked the lamplit streets of our old neighborhood in the cool of the evening. Even then, I tried to walk in stride with him. And when I caught his stride and tracked in step with him, it was such a satisfying experience. Hard to say why. Maybe it was just a young boy's game to pass the time, like counting seams in the sidewalk. But maybe there was more to it than that.

Henry David Thoreau once wrote: "If a man does not keep pace with his companions, perhaps it is because he hears a different drummer. Let him step to the music he hears, however measured or far away."[3]

Something about being in rhythm with the music makes us feel good and whole and connected to something larger than us. Maybe that is something of what I felt as a young boy trying to keep pace with my father's steps.

Everything we do, we do rhythmically, which is to say, musically. When we walk, there is a cadence to our steps. When we dance, there is a music to our movements. When we throw a baseball, we do it with a rhythm of winding up, throwing, and following through. Whether it's a baseball player pitching or a ballerina dancing or a custodian sweeping, if they do what they do well, they do it in sync with a certain rhythm.

When they don't, the level of discord increases, and with it, their chances of failure. The ballerina may gracefully leap into the air, but if her timing is off on the way down, she may fall flat on her face. The same is true of the farmer who is in sync with the planting season but maybe out of sync with the harvest. If he is late in getting to the fields, the crop may be ruined. If we want to live in harmony with the universe as God has ordered it, we must live our lives in response to those rhythms.

But there are other rhythms at work in the universe.

From the heart of God comes the strongest rhythm—the rhythm of love. Without His love reverberating in us, whatever we do will come across like a noisy gong or a clanging symbol. And so the work of the human heart, it seems to me, is to listen for that music and pick up on its rhythms.

In his autobiographical novel, *A River Runs Through It*, Norman Maclean described his father as a Scot and a Presbyterian minister who believed that man by nature was a mess and had fallen from an original state of grace, and that "only by picking up on God's rhythms were we able to regain power and beauty."[4]

King David's life had become such a mess in his adultery with Bathsheba and the murder of her husband. Once a person who composed music that soothed the troubled soul of Saul, David had fallen into a life of discord. When he called out, "Create in me a pure heart, O God, and renew a steadfast spirit within me," it was an attempt to bring his life back in harmony with God's rhythms.

Our Father's Will

Jesus spent His life listening for that music and living in harmony with its rhythms. From the beginning of Christ's life to His death, He was always in step with His Father, every step keeping pace, stride for stride. Follow Jesus through the Gospels and you get a sense of that stride. Walk with Him through a couple of chapters of John, for example. In the story of the Samaritan woman in chapter four, Jesus met her at a well just outside the town of Sychar, and, because of her, many of the townspeople became believers. In the next chapter, Jesus came to the pool of Bethesda, a huge place with five covered colonnades and people with all sorts of infirmities surrounding it. But Jesus did not heal everyone there, only one man, a man who had been an invalid for thirty-eight years.

In one chapter, a multitude of people were touched by Christ. In the very next chapter, only one. Why? Because in Samaria the Father was doing a very big thing. In Bethesda, He was doing a very small thing. Jesus' idea of success had nothing to do with numbers or performance or living up to some human standard. His idea of success was simply doing His Father's will. "Truly, truly I say to you," Jesus said, "the Son can do nothing of Himself, unless it is something He sees the Father doing; for whatever the Father does, these things the Son also does in like manner" (John 5:19).

Which is another way of saying, He listened to the beat of a different drummer, and He stepped to the music He heard, however measured or far away. A life like that cannot be lived by following someone else's steps to successful living. It can only be lived by following the Father's steps.

Christ's healing of a lame man at the pool of Bethesda caused a controversy because it was the Sabbath. The Jews felt the healing qualified as work, therefore violating their religious law. Christ's response to His critics? "My Father is always at work to this very day, and I, too, am working" (v. 17). The steps of Jesus' life kept pace with His Father's.

Which put Him out of step with His companions.

He asks no less of us. When He tells us to walk the extra mile, Jesus is asking us to fall out-of-step with the world and in-step with the faraway drumbeat of heaven. When He tells us to turn the other cheek, to give up our cloak if we are sued, He is trying to bring our earthly lives in harmony with the eternal rhythms pulsing from the Father's heart.

Now and then we hear something of the music that Jesus heard so clearly and so regularly. How? The Holy Spirit resides in us like the strings of a finely tuned instrument, which resonates with the music. Sometimes lyrics accompany the music. Other times we hear only the tune, and the Spirit within us senses it, reverberating with a certainty beyond the ability of words to capture.

Our Father's Call

C.S. Lewis captured the fleeting nature of this music when he wrote: "All the things that have ever deeply possessed your soul have been but hints of it—tantalizing glimpses, promises never quite fulfilled, echoes that died away just as they caught your ear. But if it should really become manifest— if there ever came an echo that did not die away but swelled into the sound itself—you would know it. Beyond all possibility of doubt you would say 'Here at last is the thing I was made for.'"[5]

When we live our lives with an inner stillness, the way a weaned child rests against its mother, we get a sense not only of oneness with the Father but a certainty of His purpose for our life.

Albert Schweitzer was certain of God's purpose for his life. That certainty, though, came only after years of reflection. "Many a time already had I tried to settle what meaning lay hidden for me in the saying of Jesus! 'Whosoever would lose his life for My sake and the Gospels shall save it.' Now the answer was found. In addition to the outward, I now have inward happiness.

"What would be the character of the activities thus planned for the future was not yet clear to me. Only one thing was certain, that it must be directly human service, however inconspicuous the sphere of it."

Only after much prayer and reflection did it become clear to Schweitzer that he was to leave the academic halls of Europe for the untamed jungles of Africa. That was his calling, he felt certain. Losing his life is what God wanted him to do. Africa is where He wanted him to it. There he served with an inconspicuous kind of love, his life an example of the fruit that can come forth when the Word of God is given a place in our heart to grow.

When we know our gifting, our calling, that thing we were made for, we can serve God more effectively because there is less wasted motion to our activity. Love, joy, and peace are just some of the fruit.

Love comes while we rest against our Father's chest.

Joy comes when we catch the rhythms of His heart.

Peace comes when we live in harmony with those rhythms.

It is within the closeness and warmth of that relationship where we gain the certainty that we are doing the very thing He would have us do with our lives. Whether that thing is motherhood or sainthood, God only knows. But if we crawl onto His lap, lay our head against His chest, and listen . . . He will tell us.

PART VIII

The Harvest of the Reflective Life

Whatever a man sows, this will he also reap. For the one who sows to his own flesh shall from the flesh reap corruption, but the one who sows to the Spirit shall from the Spirit reap eternal life. And let us not lose heart in doing good, for in due time we shall reap if we do not grow weary. So then, while we have opportunity, let us do good to all men, and especially to those who are of the household of the faith.

GALATIANS 6:7-10

E ach piece of fruit has within it the seeds of its own reproduction. It was designed that way so that each harvest could seed the next, so that no generation would ever be without food.

I would like to end the book with a story about such a harvest.

To introduce the story, here's a final film clip from *The Shawshank Redemption*. The movie is about prisoners in the Shawshank prison, struggling to hold on to their humanity. Andy, played by Tim Robbins, is there struggling too. He carves chessmen from stone, petitions the state for books for the prison library, and helps inmates get their high school diploma. These are a few of the ways he holds on to his humanity. One other way costs him two weeks in solitary confinement when he gains access to the prison's public address system and plays a record for the entire prison to hear.

As the music streams through the washroom and prison yard, the inmates stop and stand transfixed. The actor, Morgan Freeman, a friend of Andy's and narrator of the story, says these words about that moment: "I have no idea to this day what those two Italian ladies were singing about. Truth is, I don't wanna know. Some things are best left unsaid. I'd like to think they were singing about something so beautiful it can't be expressed in words and makes your heart ache because of it. I tell you those voices soared, higher and farther than anybody in the great place dared to dream. It was like some beautiful bird flapped into Alexander's cage and made those walls dissolve away. And for the briefest of moments, every last man at Shawshank felt free."

That is the power of music, the power to pass through prison bars, break apart chains, open the cell that has incarcerated the soul, and liberate it.

I felt the power of that music when I was in high school. And it wasn't at a Rolling Stones concert.

I grew up in Fort Worth, Texas, and attended Arlington Heights High School in the late '60s, when the Beatles, the Doors, the Rolling Stones, and anybody else with a drum and an electric guitar produced a lot of powerful music. I heard that music throbbing out of car windows from 8-tracks in the parking lot and reverberating from oversized speakers at school dances. But that was not the music that liberated me.

The music that liberated me was softer, quieter. I heard it one day on campus at the end of my junior year. On that spring day in 1968, Christ showed up.

He showed up in a pair of Converse All-Stars, gym shorts, T-shirt, a handshake, and a smile. Several of us on the basketball team were playing a pickup game in the gym, and this young seminary student from Southwestern Baptist Theological Seminary worked his way into the game. Over the weeks ahead he kept showing up. At lunch. After school. In the parking lot. And before long, he worked his way into our lives.

His name was Scott Manley.

He talked several of us into going to summer camp, and it was, as he promised, the best week of our lives. The following year I got more involved with Young Life, attending weekly club meetings, a Bible study called Campaigners, and the next summer I went to a Young Life college prep camp at Star Ranch.

There, during a 20-minute quiet time after the last message, I gave what little I knew of my life to what little I knew of Christ's. It wasn't much, I told Him, but what I had was His, if He wanted it, or if in some way He could use it.

In the fall I attended Texas Christian University, where I got involved with Young Life leadership. By my sophomore year I was leading a Young Life club and was involved in weekly leadership meetings. From that leadership group came many of my dear friends. And one who is my dearest.

Her name is Judy.

She had been introduced to Christ by a classmate who had become a Christian through her Young Life leader, who had become a Christian through my Young Life leader, Scott Manley.

I don't recall any of the talks Scott gave at club meetings or in Campaigners. I don't remember the lyrics, but the music, the music I'll never forget.

The music streamed into my ears, saying, *I love you. I care about you. You matter. Your pain matters. Your struggles matter. Your life is sacred and dear to God. He has a future for you, plans and hopes and dreams for you, and blessings for you.*

My wife had never met Scott, although she had heard the stories from several of us who had been touched by him. She had thought a long time about what she would say if and when she ever did meet him. She had rehearsed it in her mind over and over again.

Two years ago, she finally met him. We were attending a conference with some friends and three of our four children. He had been introduced by the speaker, who also had come to Christ in high school through Scott. After the meeting, Judy gathered the children and searched him out in the crowd.

When she found him, she said: "You don't know me, but I'm Judy Gire, Ken Gire's wife." They hugged, then she continued. "There's something I've been wanting to tell you for a long time." Years of waiting emotion welled inside her. "Scott, you were instrumental in leading my husband to Christ.

You led my Young Life leader to Christ. My Young Life leader led a friend of mine to Christ. And this friend told me about Christ. You are my spiritual heritage. These are three of our four children. This is Kelly, and she knows Jesus. This is Rachel, and she knows Jesus. This is Stephen, and he knows Jesus. And Gretchen, our oldest, she isn't here, but she knows Jesus, too. All of us know Jesus because of Scott Manley. Thank you so much. Thank you."

Scott threw his arms around her, and together and for a long time they wept.

That is a picture of the love of God and how it was meant to spill over into the lives of those around us.

To us it has been given the greatest song in all the universe to sing.

It isn't important we sing it professionally, with great polish.

But it is important we sing it passionately, with great heart.

When we come together as Christians, united by our love for God and for our neighbor, that is when we will be in harmony with the melody of the Father's heart. And that is when our lives will become a song so beautiful it will make the entire world stop and listen.

Maybe they won't understand the words. And maybe after hearing them, they will simply return to what they were doing before. Even so, they will sense that what they have heard comes from someplace higher and farther than any of them have dared to dream. And for the briefest of moments, the heart of every last person who hears it will ache to be free.

So until Jesus returns, we sing.

Together.

In harmony.

And when at last He appears, the most passionate notes we have sung here on earth will seem only the humming of a prelude. And we will discover, some of us maybe for the first time, that the sad and sometimes somber notes of our lives here on earth were in fact the deep, visceral strains of a great, heavenly symphony.

And when we see Jesus, the one whom we have loved only from afar, we will burst into song, tears streaming down our faces, never wanting the song to end, each stanza lifting us higher to fuller expressions of love for Him who sounded the first and most beautiful note that gave us all not only a reason to live . . .

but to sing.

ENDNOTES

INTRODUCTION

1. Mary Ann Evans, *Nell*, New York: Berkley Books, 1995, pp. 242-43.

PART I. THE REFLECTIVE LIFE

1. Thomas R. Kelly, *A Testament of Devotion*, New York: Harper & Brothers, 1941, p. 115.

THE SACREDNESS OF LIFE

1. Abraham Joshua Heschel, *Man Is Not Alone: A Philosophy of Religion*, New York: Farrar, Straus & Giroux, 1951, p. 227.

2. Abraham Joshua Heschel, *God in Search of Man: A Philosophy of Judaism*, New York: Farrar, Straus & Giroux, 1955, p. 74.

3. Ernest Thompson Seton, *The Gospel of the Redman*, London: Methuen & Co., Ltd., 1937, p. 1.

4. Ibid., pp. 76-77.

5. Ibid., p. 18.

6. Ibid., p. 286.

SLOWING DOWN TO SEE WHAT IS SACRED

1. Jean-Pierre De Caussade, *The Sacrament of the Present Moment*, San Francisco: HarperSanFrancisco, 1981, p. 80.

2. Abraham Joshua Heschel, *Man Is Not Alone: A Philosophy of Religion*, New York: Farrar, Straus & Giroux, 1951, p. 165.

3. Abraham Joshua Heschel, *God in Search of Man: A Philosophy of Judaism*, New York: Farrar, Straus & Giroux, 1955, p. 78.

4. Ernest Thompson Seton, *The Gospel of the Redman*, London: Methuen & Co., Ltd., 1937, p. 60.

5. Abraham J. Heschel, *Who Is Man?* Stanford, CA: Stanford University Press, 1965, p. 24.

6. Ann Tusa and John Tusa, *The Nuremberg Trial*, New York: Atheneum, 1984, p. 167.

PART II. THE SEED OF THE REFLECTIVE LIFE

1. Thomas Merton, *Seeds of Contemplation*, (no city), A New Directions Book, 1949, p. 17.

2. Frederick Buechner, *A Room Called Remember*, San Francisco: Harper & Row Publishers, 1984, p. 13.

PART III. THE SOIL OF THE REFLECTIVE LIFE

1. Andrew Murray, *Humility*, Springdale, PA: Whitaker House, 1982, p. 102.

PART IV. THE WATER OF THE REFLECTIVE LIFE

1. Morton Kelsey, *Prayer and the Redwood Seed*, Rockport, Massachusetts: Element, 1991, pp. 49-50.

2. A.W. Tozer, *The Pursuit of God*, Camp Hill, PA: Christian Publications, Inc., 1982, pp. 80-81.

3. Geoffrey C. Ward with Ric Burns and Ken Burns, *The Civil War*, New York: Alfred A. Knopf, Inc., 1990, pp. 82-83.

PART V. THE CULTIVATION OF THE REFLECTIVE LIFE

1. Judith Handelsman, *Growing Myself: A Spiritual Journey Through Gardening*, New York: Dutton, 1996, pp. 129-130.

GOD'S MISSION STATEMENT FOR OUR LIFE

1. Stephen R. Covey, *The 7 Habits of Highly Effective People*, New York: Simon & Schuster, 1989, p. 108.

HABITS OF THE HEART THAT HEIGHTEN OUR SPIRITUAL SENSES

1. Guigo, *The Ladder of Monks*, quoted in *Ways of Imperfection* by Simon Tugwell, Springfield, IL: Templegate Publishers, 1985, p. 99.

2. *The Thoughts of Thoreau*, edited by Edwin Way Teale, New York: Dodd, Mead, and Company, 1962, p. 231.

3. Ken Gire, *Windows of the Soul*, Grand Rapids, MI: Zondervan Publishing House, 1996, pp. 27-37.

PART VI. THE GROWTH OF THE REFLECTIVE LIFE

1. James Allen, *As a Man Thinketh*, (no city), Fleming H. Revell Company, (no date), p. 15.

REFLECTING ON THE SCRIPTURES

1. Richard Foster, *Celebration of Discipline*, San Francisco: Harper & Row Publishers,

1988, pp. 29-30.

2. Henri J.M. Nouwen, *Reaching Out*, New York: Doubleday, 1975, pp. 35-36.

3. Anne Morrow Lindbergh, *Gift from the Sea*, New York: Pantheon Books, Inc., 1955, p. 29.

4. Thomas R. Kelly, *A Testament of Devotion*, New York: Harper & Brothers, 1941, p. 118.

5. Ken Gire, *Moments with the Savior*, Grand Rapids, MI: Zondervan Publishing House, 1998, pp. 209-210.

6. Dietrich Bonhoeffer, *Life Together*, New York: Harper & Row Publishers, 1954, p. 83.

REFLECTING ON MOVIES

1. Marsha Sinetar, *Reel Power: Spiritual Growth Through Film*, Ligouri, Missouri: Triumph Books, 1993, pp. 21-22.

2. C.S. Lewis, *Experiment in Criticism*, London: Cambridge University Press, 1961, p. 88.

3. "Picture Perfect," *Life* : Diana: Portraits of a Lady, November 1997, 14.

4. Michael Satchell, "Death Comes to a Living Saint," *U.S. News & World Report*, 15 September 1997, 12.

REFLECTING ON OTHER PEOPLE

1. Frederick Buechner, *The Magnificent Defeat*, San Francisco: Harper & Row Publishers, 1966, pp. 48-49.

2. Norman C. Habel, *For Mature Adults Only*, Philadelphia: Fortress Press, 1969, pp. 82-83.

3. Mary Murphy, "Madonna Confidential," *TV Guide*, April 11, 1998, Vol. 46, No. 15, Issue #2350, p. 21.

REFLECTING ON THE THEATER

1. W.T. Price, "The Technique of Drama," quoted in *Self-Culture for Young People*, Andrew Sloan Draper, editor-in-chief, New York: Twentieth Century Self-Culture Association, Vol X, *Music, The Fine Arts, and the Drama*, 1907, p. 278.

2. Edward Behr, *The Complete Book of Les Misérables*, New York: Arcade Publishing, 1989, p. 168.

3. Ibid., p. 168.

4. Ibid., p. 186.

5. Ibid., p. 191.

6. Ibid.

7. Ibid.

8. George MacDonald, *An Anthology*, ed. by C.S. Lewis, London: Fount Paperbacks, 1946, p. 92.

PART VII. THE FRUIT OF THE REFLECTIVE LIFE

1. Thomas R. Kelly, A Testament of Devotion, New York: Harper & Brothers, 1941, pp. 123-124.

2. *Light from Many Lamps*, ed. by Lillian Eichler Watson, New York: Simon and Schuster, 1951, pp. 33-34.

3. *Thoreau: Walden and Other Writings*, ed. by Joseph Wood Krutch, New York: Bantam, 1962, p. 345.

4. Norman Maclean, *A River Runs Through It and Other Stories*, Chicago: University of Chicago Press, 1976, p. 2.

5. C.S. Lewis, *The Problem of Pain*, New York: The Macmillan Company, 1962, p. 146.

Appendix A and Appendix B are designed to introduce you to the companion books in this series. The excerpts will acquaint you with practical tools to help you live a more reflective life. These tools can make the habits of the heart—*reading the moment, reflecting on the moment,* and *responding to the moment*—as natural and necessary a part of your spiritual journey as breathing is to your physical existence.

APPENDIX A

Reflections *on the* Word

DEVOTIONAL

Meditating on God's Word in the
Everyday Moments of Life

The Bible begins and ends in Paradise. In between the garden of Eden and the garden in the New Jerusalem lies a sprawling landscape.

In the life of Israel, the landscape stretches from Ur to Egypt, winds around Mount Sinai, through a wilderness, into a land flowing with milk and honey, out into exile, and eventually back to Palestine.

The life of Christ traces other terrain. There is a wilderness, too, only a different one. And heavenly words are also revealed on a mountain, only not on tablets of stone but in words of a sermon, words that give those spoken on Mount Sinai even greater resonance. On another mountain, a higher mountain, His glory is revealed. There is a valley through which He passes, a garden in which He prays, and a hill on which He dies.

The life of the church has its own unique landscape. The peaks of Pentecost. The valleys of Corinth. The plateaus of Laodicea.

Our own lives, yours and mine, pass through a similar geography of the soul, with its pinnacles of faith and its valleys of doubt, its plateaus of complacency, its wildernesses of spiritual dryness.

Along the way, God speaks. In the peak experiences of our lives. In the valleys. On the plateaus. Even in the wilderness, where all traces of Him seem to have vanished. And who knows but that what we hear along the way may be just the word we need at that particular juncture of our spiritual journey. To walk us through some fearful valley to a place of pasture. To lead us out of some wilderness so we can lie down by still waters.

To help find out how God may be speaking to you, I have tried to encourage you in the art of meditating on His Word. For if you learn to hear Him there, you will likely learn to hear Him elsewhere.

He has much to say, not only from the Scriptures but from the circumstances of our everyday lives. However prosaic the pages of our lives may seem at first reading, within the lines or in between the lines God may be speaking. Every book we read, every movie we see, every person we talk with, every song we listen to, every moment in our lives, in fact, should be subjects for reflection and could be ways through which God is speaking.

If we travel too fast, though, we'll likely miss it. So if we want to hear what the Word of God is saying to us, first we have to slow down. That is what the format of *Reflections on the Word* is designed to do. To create pauses for reflection. The pauses are something like park benches so you can stop and sit and reflect on your own spiritual journey. To check the map. And your bearings. And to make any adjustments in your course.

We'll start each daily devotional with "*Reading* the Word." That will be followed by a section called "*Reflecting* on the Word" which offers insight into the biblical passage. Written by people from around the world and across the centuries, these insights come from such spiritual guides as Richard Foster or

Mother Teresa, A.W. Tozer or C.S. Lewis, Frederick Buechner or Philip Yancey, Edith Schaeffer or Eugene Peterson. The goal here is not academic analysis but spiritual illumination, to raise the lamp of the Word a little higher so it will shine a little brighter on whatever path you are presently traveling.

The section labeled "*Responding* to the Word" takes the reading and the reflection and makes them personal, allowing your time in the Word to find its way into your life. The prayer is designed only to start you praying, in hopes that the Holy Spirit will bring other things to mind, other vistas He would have you see, other paths He would have you take, other precipices He would have you avoid.

By allowing these spiritual guides to accompany you on your own journey, you will be mentored along the way in the art of biblical meditation. Sit with them on that park bench for a few minutes, and when you do, still your heart to listen. For sometimes the voice of God thunders into our lives, but, more often than not, it wisps by us like a gentle breeze with a fragrant reminder in it of faraway fields.

So take your time, relax, and reflect . . .

　　　not only on the biblical landscape

　　　　　but on the landscape of your life.

Reading the Word

As the deer pants for streams of water,

so my soul pants for you, O God.

My soul thirsts for God, for the living God.

(Psalm 42:1-2, NIV)

Reflecting on the Word

Our longings for God may not be as ravenous as David's, but they are as real. Because the hunger hurts, though, we try to take the edge off it in any way we can. One of those ways is with religious activity. And that can include the activity of reading books, listening to tapes, or going to seminars. Through these things, which are often very good things, even nourishing things, we are fed the experiences of others. But they are not our experiences. I can read a psalm about David crying out from a cave in the wilderness, and I should read that psalm, but it is not my psalm. It is not my psalm because it is not my cave, not my wilderness, and not my tears.

For so long in my life I expected my experience of God to be like one of those psalms, structured with pleasing rhythms, full of poetic images, a thing of beauty and grace. What I learned is that those psalms were borne out of great hunger—a hunger that no food on this earth can satisfy.

"He who is satisfied has never truly craved," said Abraham Heschel, and he said this, I think, because he knew that heaven's richest food does not satisfy our longings but rather intensifies them.

Ken Gire

Windows of the Soul

Responding to the Word

O God, I have tasted Thy goodness, and it has both satisfied me and made me thirsty for more. I am painfully conscious of my need of further grace. I am ashamed of my lack of desire. O God, the Triune God, I want to want Thee; I long to be filled with longing; I thirst to be made more thirsty still.

A.W. Tozer

The Pursuit of God

Reading the Word

An angel of the Lord appeared to him in a dream, saying, "Joseph, son of David, do not be afraid to take Mary as your wife; for that which has been conceived in her is of the Holy Spirit. And she will bear a Son; and you shall call His name Jesus, for it is He who will save His people from their sins." Now all this took place that what was spoken by the Lord through the prophet might be fulfilled, saying, "Behold, the virgin shall be with child, and shall bear a Son, and they shall call His name Immanuel," which translated means, "God with us." *(Matthew 1:20-23)*

Reflecting on the Word

The implications of the name Immanuel are both comforting and unsettling. Comforting, because He has come to share the danger as well as the drudgery of our everyday lives. He desires to weep with us and to wipe away our tears. And what seems most bizarre, Jesus Christ, the Son of God, longs to share in and to be the source of the laughter and the joy we all too rarely know.

The implications are unsettling. It is one thing to claim that God looks down upon us, from a safe distance, and speaks to us (via long distance, we hope). But to say that He is right here, is to put ourselves and Him in a totally new situation. He is no longer the calm and benevolent observer in the sky, the kindly old caricature with the beard. His image becomes that of Jesus, who wept and laughed, who fasted and feasted, and who, above all, was fully present to those He loved. He was there with them. He is here with us. . . .

He is with us in the midst of our daily, routine lives. In the middle of cleaning the house or driving somewhere in the pickup. . . . Often it's in the middle of the most mundane task that He lets us know He is there with us. We realize, then, that there can be no "ordinary" moments for people who live their lives with Jesus.

Michael Card

The Name of the Promise Is Jesus

Responding to the Word

You speak, Lord, to all men in general through general events. Revolutions are simply the tides of your Providence, which stir up storms and tempests in people's minds. You speak to men in particular through particular events, as they occur moment by moment. But instead of hearing your voice, instead of respecting events as signals of your loving guidance, people see nothing else but blind chance and human decision. They find objections to everything you say. They wish to add to or subtract from your Word. They wish to change and reform it.

Teach me, dear Lord, to read clearly this book of life. I wish to be like a simple child, accepting your word regardless of whether I understand your purposes. It is enough for me that you speak.

Jean-Pierre De Caussade

Reading the Word

Blessed are those who mourn, for they shall be comforted.
(Matthew 5:4)

Reflecting on the Word

Look back at those hours which passed over your life so calmly and contentedly. . . . If the whole of your life had been a succession of hours like those, do you know what would have become of you? You would become selfish, hardhearted, lonely, without regard for higher things, for the pure, for God—and you would never have felt blessedness. When did it first dawn on you that we men don't live unto ourselves? When did the blessedness of compassion bring comfort to you? In suffering. Where did your heart come close to those who were so distant and cold to you? In suffering. Where did you catch a glimpse of the higher destiny of your life? In suffering. Where did you feel God was near to you? In suffering. Where did you first realize the blessedness of having a Father in heaven? In suffering.

Albert Schweitzer

Reverence for Life

Responding to the Word

Dear Jesus,

Thank you for the hard and sometimes uphill road I have had to walk in following you. I am stronger because of it. And we are closer because of it. For all the good things that have come to me along the way, I thank you.

But I have to say, I wish it were an easier way,

a shorter way,

a more scenic way.

I wish the road didn't have to go past the garden of Gethsemane, with its darkness and loneliness and tears.

I wish it just went in endless circles around the seashores of Galilee, and that walking with you were more of a serene stroll in the sunset.

Help me to understand that Gethsemane is as necessary as Galilee in the geography of a growing soul.

Help me to remember that even though you were a son, yet you learned obedience through the things you suffered.

Paul talks about entering into the fellowship of your suffering. I do so very much look forward to having fellowship with you, but honestly, Lord, the thought of having to suffer to experience it stops me in my tracks.

Help me, Lord Jesus, to want your company more than I want serenity, and to love the fellowship with you more than I fear the suffering necessary to enter into it.

Ken Gire

Reading the Word

"Look at the birds, free and unfettered, not tied down to a job description, careless in the care of God. And you count far more to him than birds."
(Matthew 6:26, TM)

Reflecting on the Word

Careless in the care of God. And why shouldn't they be?

For their food, He provides insects in the air, seeds on the ground.

For their search for food, He provides eyes that are keen, wings that are swift.

For their drinking, He provides poolings of rainwater.

For their bathing, He provides puddles.

For their survival, He provides migratory instincts to take

them to warmer climates.

For their flight, He provides bones that are porous and lightweight.

For their warmth, He provides feathers.

For their dryness, He provides a water-resistant coating.

For their rest, He provides warm updrafts so they

can glide through the air.

For their journey, He provides the company of other travelers.

For their return, He provides the companionship of a mate.

For their safety, He provides a perch in branches far from the reach of predators.

For their nest, He provides twigs.

And for every newborn beak, He provides enough worms so they can grow up

to leave the nest and continue the cycle of life.

It's no wonder they're so free from the cares of this world.

The wonder is, if we count more to Him than birds, why aren't we?

Ken Gire

Responding to the Word

Grant unto us, almighty God,

the peace of God that passeth understanding,

That we, amid the storms and troubles of this our life,

may rest in thee, knowing that all things are in thee;

Not beneath thine eye only, but under thy care,

governed by thy will, guarded by thy love,

So that with a quiet heart we may see the storms of life,

the cloud and the thick darkness,

Ever rejoicing to know that the darkness and the light

are both alike to thee. . . .

George Dawson

Reading the Word

They brought to the Pharisees him who was formerly blind. Now it was the Sabbath on the day when Jesus made the clay, and opened his eyes. Again, therefore, the Pharisees also were asking him how he received his sight. And he said to them, "He applied clay to my eyes, and I washed, and I see." Therefore some of the Pharisees were saying, "This man is not from God, because He does not keep the Sabbath." But others were saying, "How can a man who is a sinner perform such signs?" And there was a division among them. . . . He therefore answered, "Whether He is a sinner, I do not know; one thing I do know, that, whereas I was blind, now I see." *(John 9:13-16, 25)*

Reflecting on the Word

Agnes Sanford says: "Religion is an experience of God. Theology is merely an attempt to explain the experience."

Well, who needs it (except the theologians)? What most of us really need is the experience. And for me, at least, theology can actually hinder, get between. Theology is like trying to enjoy the rainbow with somebody at your side analyzing it for you. Or it's like thrilling to a poem and then having some teacher tear it apart. Or Robert Frost's "Stopping by the Woods on a Snowy Evening," which John Ciardi took five thousand words to explain . . . and Frost's amusement: "Gee, I didn't know I'd meant all that." Critics and theologians can read all sorts of meanings into things even an author never intended.

So I think it must be with God, who must stand back in amazement sometimes at the tomes of literature written to "explain" religion to the masses. As if we are too dumb to understand our own experience.

Marjorie Holmes

How Can I Find You, God?

Responding to the Word

I no longer want just to hear about you, beloved Lord, through messengers. I no longer want to hear doctrines about you, nor to have my emotions stirred by people speaking of you. I yearn for your presence.

These messengers simply frustrate and grieve me, because they remind me of how distant I am from you. They reopen wounds in my heart, and they seem to delay your coming to me.

From this day onwards please send me no more messengers, no more doctrines, because they cannot satisfy my overwhelming desire for you.

I want to give myself completely to you.

And I want you to give yourself completely to me.

The love which you show in glimpses, reveal to me fully. The love which you convey through messengers, speak it to me directly. I sometimes think you are mocking me by hiding yourself from me. Come to me with the priceless jewel of your love.

St. John of the Cross

APPENDIX B

Reflections *on* Your Life

J O U R N A L

D i s c e r n i n g   t h e   V o i c e   o f   G o d

i n   t h e   E v e r y d a y   M o m e n t s   o f   L i f e

The journal is arranged so you can organize your entries either chronologically or top-
ically. The topics covered are: moments of everyday life, moments in prayer, moments
in the Scriptures, moments at work, moments with others, moments in nature,
moments of awe, moments in church, moments with the arts, moments of joy,
moments of tears, moments of the past, moments of God's silence, and moments of
waiting. What follows is a sampling of some of those moments.

INTRODUCTION

In his journal of the time he spent at Walden Pond, Henry David
Thoreau explained his reasons for going. "I went to the woods because I
wished to live deliberately, to front only the essentials of life, and see if I
could not learn what it had to teach, and not, when I came to die, discover
that I had not lived."

The purpose of this journal is the same, to help us live deliberately, reducing life to its essentials in order to learn what it has to teach.

Why?

Because when our lives are over, none of us wants to look back and see only
the time clock we've punched or the pages of the calendar we've torn off. We

want more out of life than that. Thoreau certainly wanted more. In his journal he wrote, "I wanted to live deep and suck out all the marrow of life."

Isn't that what we all want? Isn't that what Jesus wants for us? Or what else could He have meant when He said, "I have come that you might have life and that you might have it abundantly"?

To experience life more abundantly, we are going to embark on an experiment similar to Thoreau's. Except we are not going into the woods to do it. We are going into *the world.* Our average, ordinary, workaday world. The world where an alarm starts the day. The world where during the day we all have to keep track of the time. And where at the end of the day we have to set the alarm and get things ready to do it all again tomorrow. It is the world where we all must go not only to make a living but somehow to make a life.

But how are we to make a life in such a world? How are we to learn what God has to teach us when the traffic in that world is so noisy? How are we to see God at work in our lives when our foot is heavy on the pedal and everything passes by in a blur? How are we to stop and be good Samaritans when our road to Jericho is a freeway?

How?

We do it in our world the same way Thoreau did it at Walden.

Deliberately.

We have to make some deliberate decisions to slow down on the roads we're traveling, to stop at the intersections, to look and to listen. We have to read the road signs, reflect on what they're saying, and respond. Sometimes that means getting off the freeway to take another way. Sometimes that means stopping to render aid to someone who needs help. Sometimes that means coming to a complete stop to avoid an accident.

Reflections on Your Life is designed to put a few speed bumps in our day, slowing us down long enough so we can read some of those signs.

Stop at those moments where you feel God may be speaking to you. Jot down what happened, whether it was a moment in the Scriptures or a moment at the grocery store. Whether it was a scene from a movie or something from a sermon. Whether it was an article in the morning paper or a story on the evening news. Something someone said . . . or didn't say.

Then take the time to reflect upon that moment. Respond in a prayerful way by reaching up to God, then in a personal way by reaching out to the people around you.

The journal will focus on topics aimed at heightening your awareness of such moments in your own life. To give resonance to the topics, I have quoted from some of the authors who have, through their books, served as mentors to me in learning to discern the voice of God in my own life. I hope the quotes will not only introduce you to some refreshing thinkers but also encourage you to investigate their writings more fully.

Although the topics are structured, it's important to understand that the moments are not. That's because the moments are spontaneous. We can prepare our heart to receive them, but we cannot plan when or where or how we will hear them. They cannot be predicted, only anticipated. And they cannot be manipulated. They can only be received or not received. That is our only choice.

This journal is a tool to help you become more receptive to those moments. To guide you along the way, I have written down some introductory thoughts at the beginning of each section followed by a moment in which I have sensed God leading me, prompting me, or speaking to me about my life.

Those moments have helped me realize that God is there, that He sees, that He hears, that He cares. And that He is not silent. "He is," as A.W. Tozer said, "by His nature, continuously articulate. He fills the world with His speaking voice."

I hope this journal helps you hear that voice, especially the words He is speaking to you.

MOMENTS OF EVERYDAY LIFE

When God created the earth, it was a magnificent ecosystem for all the life He placed there. For the creatures that dwelt in the oceans. For those that dwelt in the skies. And for those that dwelt on the land.

As a dwelling for man, the masterpiece of creation, God designed a special place. A garden. It was an architectural triumph of both form and function, for it not only provided food and shelter for the body, it provided beauty and refreshment for the soul.

But the garden was designed to be more than a place to meet man's physical and spiritual needs. It was designed to be the ideal environment for God to cultivate His relationship with man. It was designed not only to be a bountiful place and a beautiful place, but a quiet place.

A place conducive for reflection.

Like an art gallery.

The garden was a place through which the man and woman could leisurely stroll, stopping to note the intricate design of a leaf . . . then moving on until another display stopped them, this time the exquisite colors in an orchid . . . then strolling a little farther until they came upon the branching grandeur of a tree.

The displays must have prompted questions. Who was the Artist responsible for these things? What was He like? How can we know Him?

The psalmist says that the heavens continually reveal the breathless artistry of God, that "day to day pours forth speech, and night to night reveals knowledge" (Psalm 19:1-2). Yet, as the psalmist informs us, the style of the revelation is subtle. "There is no speech, nor are there words; their voice is not heard" (v. 3).

Like an art historian walking us through the gallery, the psalmist tells us the beginning principles for understanding what we see. Whatever it is the Artist is trying to say, He is saying it through pictures not words.

If that is true, it stands to reason that the garden where man was placed was full of pictures that revealed something of who God is, what He values, how He works. Looking at some of the pictures, we can see a few of those things.

He is an *artistic* God, whose palette ranges from the most muted of colors to the most magnificent. His panache can be seen in the peacock. His plainness, in the sparrow.

He is a *powerful* God, who created tall and stately redwoods. He is also a gentle God, who delicately dotted the backs of ladybugs.

He is an *orderly* God, who values process—first the stalk, then the leaf, then the blossom, then the fruit. Yet within the creative order, there is an almost playful spontaneity. You see it in the wind that tussles a tow-headed dandelion. You see it in the whimsical twitch of a squirrel's tail. You see it in the prism of colors that sparkles from a dewdrop.

In the same way the creation reveals knowledge, so do the circumstances of our lives. The moment-by-moment events of our lives fall into the soil of our understanding like seeds. Our responsibility, like that of our first parents, is to work the garden. To prepare the soil. To tend the growth. And to take what is offered from its branches as nourishment for our soul.

Date *Oct. 10, 1997*

Every moment and every event of every man's life on earth plants something in his soul. For just as the wind carries thousands of invisible and visible winged seeds, so the stream of time brings with it germs of spiritual vitality that come to rest imperceptibly in the minds and wills of men. Most of these unnumbered seeds perish and are lost, because men are not prepared to receive them.

Thomas Merton
Seeds of Contemplation

REFLECTING ON YOUR LIFE

Reading the Moment

Sports page of USA Today. Cover story headline reads: "Smith ignores pleas, tearfully steps down." It was the press release of Dean Smith's retirement from college basketball. At 66, he is ending a 36-year career. In those 36 years, he amassed 879 wins, 2 NCAA championships, 11 trips to the final four, and a graduation rate for his players of 97.3%. The article included quotes from his players and other coaches and fans, but it was a quote from him that caused me to pause and reflect. While watching Larry Brown running the 76er's training camp at the North Carolina Dean Dome, Smith said: "Larry Brown always fires me up. I used to be like that. If I can't give this team that enthusiasm, I said I would get out. That's honestly how I feel."

Reflecting on the Moment

I've always enjoyed basketball, whether it's playing the game or watching it. No matter how busy my schedule is, I always make room for the final four at the end of March. Many of those final four games featured North Carolina, coached by Dean Smith. Like his fans, I was sorry to see him leave, but the reason he left made me respect him all the more. He didn't leave because the basketball program was in shambles and would take years to rebuild. He left because the passion he once had for the game had left him. And he knew that without that passion, he couldn't give his best. His players deserved better, he thought. So did the fans. He left, to everyone's surprise. But he left with everyone's respect.

Is there any passage of Scripture that comes to mind that sheds light on this moment?

A good name is to be more desired than great riches (Proverbs)

Responding to the Moment

Reaching up prayerfully

Father, please help me to have passion for what I do as a writer. And when the passion is gone, give me the courage and strength and integrity of a Dean Smith to make the decision to step aside so room will be made for someone who has that passion.

Reaching out personally

I'm feeling my passion waning lately. Too many commitments. Too few pauses in my life. I can't do much about it right now, but I am determined to be more careful about my schedule, because what gets crowded out in the end, is my passion for living, for writing, for other people, and for God. Judy and I have set aside Sat. mornings to go out for breakfast & talk. That's been good, and something I look forward to all week.

In humility, receive the word implanted, which is able to save your souls. (*James 1:21*)

Date

All creatures live by the hand of God. The senses can only grasp the work of man, but faith sees the work of divine action in everything. It sees that Jesus Christ lives in all things, extending his influence over the centuries so that the briefest moment and the tiniest atom contain a portion of that hidden life and its mysterious work. Jesus Christ, after his resurrection, surprised the disciples when he appeared before them in disguise, only to vanish as soon as he had declared himself. The same Jesus still lives and works among us, still surprises souls whose faith is not sufficiently pure and strong. There is no moment when God is not manifest in the form of some affliction, obligation or duty. Everything that happens to us, in us, and through us, embraces and conceals God's divine but veiled purpose, so that we are always being taken by surprise and never recognize it until it has been accomplished. If we could pierce the veil and if we were vigilant and attentive, God would unceasingly reveal himself to us and we would rejoice in his works and all that happens to us. We would say to everything: 'It is the Lord!'

Jean-Pierre De Caussade
The Sacrament of the Present Moment

REFLECTING ON YOUR LIFE

Reading the Moment

Reflecting on the Moment

Is there any passage of Scripture that comes to mind that sheds light on this moment?

Responding to the Moment

Reaching up prayerfully

Reaching out personally

But Mary was standing outside the tomb weeping; and so, as she wept, she stooped and looked into the tomb; and she beheld two angels in white sitting, one at the head, and one at the feet, where the body of Jesus had been lying. And they said to her, "Woman, why are you weeping?"

She said to them, "Because they have taken away my Lord, and I do not know where they have laid Him." When she had said this, she turned around, and beheld Jesus standing there, and did not know that it was Jesus.

Jesus said to her, "Woman, why are you weeping? Whom are you seeking?"

Supposing Him to be the gardener, she said to Him, "Sir, if you have carried Him away, tell me where you have laid Him, and I will take Him away."

Jesus said to her, "Mary!"

She turned and said to Him in Hebrew, "Rabboni!" (which means, Teacher).

Jesus said to her, "Stop clinging to Me, for I have not yet ascended to the Father; but go to My brethren, and say to them, 'I ascend to My Father and your Father, and My God and your God.'"

Mary Magdalene came, announcing to the disciples, "I have seen the Lord," and that He had said these things to her. (*John 20:11-18*)

MOMENTS WITH THE ARTS

In some circles of the church today and in some centuries of church history, the arts have been looked at suspiciously if not scornfully. But like the tarnished image of God in every human being, the tarnish is not all there is to our humanness. Underneath our fallenness is the gloriousness from which we have fallen. And if only we have the eyes to see, something of that gloriousness glints through the verdegris that covers us all.

To be sure, the arts have given us plenty of reasons to be skeptical of them, even critical of them. But they have given us something else.

They have given us moments.

Acclaimed screenwriter Robert Towne once said, "A movie, I think, is really only four or five moments between two people; the rest of it exists to give those moments their impact and resonance."

There are moments within us so joyful that dancing comes closer to capturing the feeling than anything else. There are moments so tragic that nothing but drama could begin to describe the ache. There are moments so peaceful only the rhythms of a gentle musical score could convey the feeling. There are moments so lovely only the delicate hands of a sonnet could hold its loveliness without crushing it. There are moments so fleeting only a painting could still it long enough to be touched.

Through dance, through drama, through music, through poetry, through art, the soul expresses itself. With a passionate but sometimes unsteady hand, the arts trace the distant shores of the soul, mapping its uncharted reaches, with all its promises of gold and its warnings of dragons.

The map may be marked with sightings of mermaids, which in reality were only seals basking on the rocks, seen through the eyes of delirious and sunstruck sailors. The map may be noted with superstitious symbols at its edges to steer ships away from falling off the flat surface of the earth. The map is not infallible. But it does offer direction. And it can help in our search for God and for each other and for ourselves, which is sometimes the most scary and uncertain search.

Like all searches, now and then it comes up empty-handed or with hands filled with less than we expected, but often the North on the map turns out to be true North or very close to it. And though the map may not lead us home, it may help us get our bearings.

What keeps us coming back to the arts, in spite of the disappointments, is hope. Not only the hope of touching something just out of our reach, but the hope of being touched in return. Not only the hoping of finding something, but the hope of being found. Not only the hope of loving, but the hope of being loved.

Sometimes it is the love of God that finds us there, touches us there. Through the play *Les Misérables,* maybe. Or maybe through a poignant phrase of a Simon and Garfunkel song. Or a crayoned picture taped to the refrigerator door.

Take some time this week to treat yourself to a few moments in the arts. That might be a walk through the landscape art of a botanical garden or a visit to a music store to listen to a new CD on headphones. Wherever it is you go, see if there isn't some moment there that moves you. Note where it moves you. And why.

Date _Jan. 10, 1998_

[Drama] gives the essence of life, and in three hours it speaks volumes. It warns and counsels, teaches justice and keeps alive pity. It celebrates man's liberty and his struggles, and all that is noble wanders into it. It enlists the sympathies to such an extent that the listener is his own poet. It analyzes all motives, withholding nothing, lays bare everything. It is in fact the plainest, most direct of all forms of teaching. It does not formulate morals in words, but in deeds; and if life, which is the drama, is not a constant mentor, unheeded also in its teachings, what is it?

W.T. Price
The Technique of Drama

REFLECTING ON YOUR LIFE

Reading the Moment

Saw the movie, _Titanic_, which prompted me to rent the video, _A Night to Remember_, an earlier version of the 1912 disaster. Several scenes leapt out at me, all involving the _California_, a ship that was only an hour away. It was close enough to come to Titanic's aid and rescue all on board if it had responded to the distress signals that were sent both by sky rockets and by wireless. Tragically, the people on board failed to see or hear the distress signals, resulting in the loss over 2/3 of the Titanic's passengers and crew.

Reflecting on the Moment

The tragedy of the Titanic is so epic it seems a parable of sorts for all of us who live in an era of technological marvels. The main lesson of the parable seems clear enough — how pride comes before the fall, or, in this case, before the sinking. The pride of man's mastery over his environment, causing him to go "full steam ahead" in spite of the warnings of icebergs, is what led to the collision. The pride of thinking the ship was "unsinkable" is what led to the decision not to put enough lifeboats on board. But the scenes involving the _California_ teach another lesson. The men on board had seen the sky rockets in the distance, but they took them for the fireworks of a celebration, not a distress signal. The radio operator had taken off his headphones and gone to sleep, missing the Titanic's SOS. All this underscores to me the importance of being attentive & responsive to the distress signals around me.

Is there any passage of Scripture that comes to mind that sheds light on this moment?

Pride goes before the fall. (Prov.)
You have ears but do not hear, and eyes but do not see (somewhere in O.T.)
"Lord, when did we see you hungry or thirsty or in prison?" (Matt. 25)

Responding to the Moment

Reaching up prayerfully

Please, God, help me to be awake and alert at my post as a husband, as a father, and as a friend. Help me to be able to recognize the distress signals that are going out all around me. Help me be quick to hear, diligent to see, and swift to respond.

Reaching out personally

Who are some of the people around me that are sending out distress signals for help?
① A letter came from someone who is struggling with the moral equivalent of a brush with an iceberg. I should call, not ~~not~~ write. And soon. Try to help the best I can.
② Question – Is my body sending out distress signals that I've been missing? Some trouble sleeping.
③ A boy who's a friend of our kids has a mother dying of cancer. He's very quiet so I need to be especially alert for distress signals. Keep him in my prayers. Think of ways to help him and his dad. Include him with some family things, invite him over, etc.

To you, O men, I call,
And my voice is to the sons of men.
O naive ones, discern prudence;
And, O fools, discern wisdom.
(Proverbs 8:4-5)

Date

One artist imagines himself the creator of an autonomous spiritual world; he hoists upon his shoulders the act of creating this world and of populating it, together with the total responsibility for it. . . .

Another artist recognizes above himself a higher power and joyfully works as a humble apprentice under God's heaven, though graver and more demanding still is his responsibility for all he writes or paints—and for the souls which apprehend it. However, it was not he who created this world, nor does he control it; there can be no doubts about its foundations. It is merely given to the artist to sense more keenly than others the harmony of the world, the beauty and ugliness of man's role in it—and to vividly communicate this to mankind . . . .

Archaeologists have yet to discover an earthly stage of human existence when we possessed no art. In the twilight preceding the dawn of mankind we received it from Hands which we did not have a chance to see clearly. *Why* this gift for us? How should we treat it? . . . .

Not everything can be named. Some things draw us beyond words. Art can warm even a chilled and sunless soul to an exalted spiritual experience. Through art we occasionally receive— indistinctly, briefly—revelations the likes of which cannot be achieved by rational thought.

It is like that small mirror of legend: you look into it but instead of yourself you glimpse for a moment the Inaccessible, a realm forever beyond reach. And your soul begins to ache. . . .

Aleksandr I. Solzhenitsyn
"The Nobel Lecture on Literature"
East and West

REFLECTING ON YOUR LIFE

Reading the Moment

Reflecting on the Moment

Is there any passage of Scripture that comes to mind that sheds light on this moment?

Responding to the Moment

Reaching up prayerfully

Reaching out personally

Now the Lord spoke to Moses, saying, "See, I have called by name Bezalel, the son of Uri, the son of Hur, of the tribe of Judah. And I have filled him with the Spirit of God in wisdom, in understanding, in knowledge, and in all kinds of craftsmanship, to make artistic designs for work in gold, in silver, and in bronze, and in the cutting of stones for settings, and in the carving of wood, that he make work in all kinds of craftsmanship. And behold, I Myself have appointed with him Oholiab, the son of Ahisamach, of the tribe of Dan; and in the hearts of all who are skillful I have put skill, that they may make all that I have commanded you: the tent of meeting, and the ark of testimony, and the mercy seat upon it, and all the furniture of the tent, the table also and its utensils, and the pure gold lampstand with all its utensils, and the altar of incense, the altar of burnt offering also with its utensils, and the laver and its stand, the woven garments as well, and the holy garments for Aaron the priest, and the garments of his sons, with which to carry on their priesthood; the anointing oil also, and the fragrant incense for the holy place, they are to make them according to all that I have commanded you. (*Exodus 31:1-11*)

MOMENTS OF TEARS

We cry for all sorts of reasons. When we're happy. When we're sad. When we're frustrated. When we're angry. When we're scared. When we're in pain. When we see someone else in pain.

Though the chemical composition of those tears is the same, their meaning is not.

Look up a word like *run* in the dictionary, for example, and you'll see that though the word is spelled the same in all its contexts, its meaning is different. A nose can run, and that is different from a run on a bank. And that is different from a run of salmon. And that is different from a home run. And that is different from something that is run-of-the-mill.

The tears that come to our eyes when we drop a can of beans on our foot are different from the tears that come to our eyes when we look at an old photograph and remember someone we love. And those tears are different from the ones that come to our eyes when we jump to our feet when the home team comes from behind to score the winning touchdown.

Tears are the language of the soul, and like any language, the meaning of its words are not determined by a dictionary definition but by the context in which the words are used. Sometimes the context of our tears or the tears of others lies deep within the memory of the soul. Tears have a way of taking us back in time to give attention to those memories, something in the past that needs healing, maybe, or forgiving, or understanding, or simply honoring by our grateful remembrance.

Though more difficult to define, tears are more expressive than words. They are also more difficult to hide behind than words, for what we weep over reveals who we are. Our tears pull back the curtain to reveal the identity of our true self, which is often kept from other people like a self-conscious secret.

Tears not only reveal our true self, they renew our soul, they restore us to one another, and sometimes in a watershed moment they even redirect the course of our life. Such is the power of tears.

And sometimes that power is harnessed by God as a moment of revelation.

About us.

About other people.

Even about God Himself.

Date *Spring, 1993*

You never know what may cause them. The sight of the Atlantic Ocean can do it, or a piece of music, or a face you've never seen before. A pair of somebody's old shoes can do it. Almost any movie made before the great sadness that came over the world after the Second World War, a horse cantering across a meadow, the high school basketball team running out onto the gym floor at the start of a game. You can never be sure. But of this you can be sure. Whenever you find tears in your eyes, especially unexpected tears, it is well to pay the closest attention.

They are not only telling you something about the secret of who you are, but more often than not God is speaking to you through them of the mystery of where you have come from and is summoning you to where, if your soul is to be saved, you should go next.

Frederick Buechner
Whistling in the Dark

REFLECTING ON YOUR LIFE

Reading the Moment

My daughter Kelly was graduating from middle school at a Christian school in southern California. I accompanied her to the banquet, honoring their passage into high school. It was a fairly formal affair with everyone dressed-up, taking pictures, things like that. When everyone was seated, one of the girls in the class walked to the microphone to say the blessing. She started a little shaky, her voice cracking, then pausing, and trying to start up again. It was an awkward moment, and my heart went out to her as I'm sure everyone else's did. "Please, God, help her get through this," I prayed. But she couldn't get through it. She was crying at the microphone until finally a school official came to her rescue and finished the prayer for her.

Reflecting on the Moment

It was at that moment that I knew how much the school had meant to that girl at the microphone – and to all the kids who went there, for when the prayer was finished others were wiping their eyes too. The tears of that girl that evening were more articulate and compelling than any promotional brochure I had read from the school. In those tears were distilled all the love, the friendships, the influence of the faculty, all the wonderful experiences that she was leaving behind. If I had ever ~~questioned~~ questioned whether this was a good place for my kids, I questioned no longer.

Is there any passage of Scripture that comes to mind that sheds light on this moment?

I can't think of any off hand.

Responding to the Moment

Reaching up prayerfully

Father, thank you for this school to which I have entrusted a portion of my children's lives. Thank you for the hard work and the ~~enthusiasm~~ dedication of all the teachers and the staff. Thank you for the friendships that are here and the experiences that they all have shared together, and that this is a place where the Lord Jesus is honored. Thank you for that.

Reaching out personally

Although my kids are at a different school in a different state, it is still a school where Christ is honored. I take that for granted. And I have been remiss in not expressing my appreciation. This week I will write the principal a note of appreciation, along with some notes for several of the teachers who have made a difference in my kids' lives.

Now one of the Pharisees was requesting Him to dine with him. And He entered the Pharisee's house, and reclined at the table. And behold, there was a woman in the city who was a sinner; and when she learned that He was reclining at the table in the Pharisee's house, she brought an alabaster vial of perfume, and standing behind Him at His feet, weeping, she began to wet His feet with her tears. . . . (*Luke 7:36-38a*)

Date

There is no language more compelling and expressive than tears. Among all forms of communication, crying has the potential to express the greatest variety of messages with the most captivating effects.

Jeffrey A. Kottler
The Language of Tears

REFLECTING ON YOUR LIFE

Reading the Moment

Reflecting on the Moment

Is there any passage of Scripture that comes to mind that sheds light on this moment?

Responding to the Moment

Reaching up prayerfully

Reaching out personally

When Mary came where Jesus was, she saw Him, and fell at His feet, saying to Him, "Lord, if You had been here, my brother would not have died."

When Jesus therefore saw her weeping, and the Jews who came with her, also weeping, He was deeply moved in spirit, and was troubled, and said, "Where have you laid him?"

They said to Him, "Lord, come and see."

Jesus wept. And so the Jews were saying, "Behold how He loved him!"
(John 11:32-36)

APPENDIX C

Recommended Books *to* Nurture *the* Reflective Life

There are many books that could be recommended to nurture the reflective life. The following, however, are books I have read that have helped me. If you're wanting to do further study, any of these books would be a good place to start.

Baillie, John, *A Diary of Private Prayer*, New York: Charles Scribner's Sons, 1949.

Bonhoeffer, Dietrich, *Life Together*, New York: Harper & Row, Publishers, 1954.

Buechner, Frederick, *The Sacred Journey*, San Francisco: Harper & Row, Publishers, 1982.

Buechner, Frederick, *Now and Then*, San Francisco: Harper & Row, Publishers, 1983.

Buechner, Frederick, *Telling Secrets*, San Francisco: Harper & Row, Publishers, 1991.

Buechner, Frederick, *A Room Called Remember*, San Francisco: Harper & Row, Publishers, 1984.

Buechner, Frederick, *The Clown in the Belfry*, San Francisco: HarperSanFrancisco, Publishers, 1992.

Buechner, Frederick, *The Hungering Dark*, San Francisco: Harper & Row, Publishers, 1969.

Buechner, Frederick, *Listening to Your Life*, San Francisco: HarperSanFrancisco, 1992.

Buechner, Frederick, *The Magnificent Defeat*, San Francisco: Harper & Row, Publishers, 1966.

Buechner, Frederick, *Telling the Truth: The Gospel as Tragedy, Comedy, and Fairy Tale*, San Francisco: Harper & Row, Publishers, 1977.

Buechner, Frederick, *Whistling in the Dark*, San Francisco: Harper & Row, Publishers, 1988.

Buechner, Frederick, *Wishful Thinking*, San Francisco: Harper & Row, Publishers, 1973.

De Caussade, Jean-Pierre, *The Sacrament of the Present Moment*, San Francisco: HarperSanFrancisco, 1981.

Foster, Richard, *Prayer: Finding the Heart's True Home*, San Francisco: HarperSanFrancisco, 1992.

Heschel, Abraham Joshua, *God in Search of Man: A Philosophy of Judaism*, New York: Farrar, Straus and Giroux, 1955.

Heschel, Abraham Joshua, *Man Is Not Alone: A Philosophy of Religion*, New York: Farrar, Straus and Giroux, 1951.

Holmes, Marjorie, *I've Got to Talk to Somebody, God*, New York: Doubleday and Company, 1969.

Kelly, Thomas R., *A Testament of Devotion*, New York: Harper & Brothers Publishers, 1941.

Kelsey, Morton, *Prayer & The Redwood Seed*, Rockport, Massachusetts: Element, Inc., 1991.

Kidd, Sue Monk, *When the Heart Waits*, San Francisco: Harper & Row, Publishers, 1990.

Lawrence, Brother, & Laubach, Frank, *Practicing the Presence of God*, Sargent, Georgia: The SeedSowers, 1973.

Lewis, C.S., *A Grief Observed*, New York: Bantam Books, 1976.

Lewis, C.S., *Letters to Malcolm: Chiefly on Prayer*, New York: Harcourt Brace Jovanovich, 1964.

Lindbergh, Anne Morrow, *Gift from the Sea*, New York: Pantheon, 1955.

Nouwen, Henri, *Reaching Out*, New York: Doubleday, 1975.

Nouwen, Henri, *Show Me the Way*, New York: Crossroad, 1994.

Nouwen, Henri, *The Way of the Heart*, San Francisco: HarperSanFrancisco, 1981.

Postema, Don, *Space for God*, Grand Rapids, Michigan: Bible Way, 1983.

Rilke, Rainer Maria, *Letters to a Young Poet*, New York: W. W. Norton Company, 1962.

Rilke, Rainer Maria, *Letters on Cézanne*, New York: Fromm International Publishing Company, 1985.

Thoreau, Henry David, *Thoreau: Walden and Other Writings*, New York: Bantam Books, 1962.

Tozer, A. W., *The Pursuit of God*, Camp Hill, Pennsylvania: Christian Publications, Inc., 1982.

Mars Hill Review is an excellent periodical of essays, studies, and reminders of God. Subscriptions can be ordered by calling 1-800-990-MARS or by writing to: Mars Hill Review, 11757 W. Ken Caryl F330, Littleton, CO 80127-3700.

NURTURING A MORE REFLECTIVE WAY OF WATCHING MOVIES

Following are a couple of people who have helped me look at movies more reflectively, which in turn helped me look at life more reflectively. The first one is Linda Seger. Linda is a script consultant in Hollywood, a Christian, and she consulted with me on a screenplay I wrote titled, *McKinney High, 1946*. I heartily recommend all of her books.

The Art of Adaptation, New York: Henry Holt and Company, 1992.

Creating Unforgettable Characters, New York: Henry Holt and Company, 1990.

Linda Seger and Edward J. Whetmore, *From Script to Screen*, New York: Henry Holt and Company, 1994.

Making a Good Script Great, New York: Dodd, Mead & Company, 1987.

The second person who helped me to observe film in greater depth is Pauline Kael. For years she was a film critic for *The New Yorker*, and the reviews she published in that magazine have been collected in book form.

She is a severe critic and seems rarely ever to like a movie, but her criticism is insightful, discussing everything from the acting to the directing to the writing, down to the slightest details of lighting and set design. Below are a few of her books.

Hooked, New York: E.P. Dutton, 1989.

Movie Love, New York: Penguin Books, 1991.

Taking It All In, New York: Holt, Rinehart and Winston, 1984.